THE VICTIM MENTALITY DEFEATED

Michael Lewis Moore

ACKNOWLEDGMENTS AND DEDICATION

I would never have attempted this book without the encouragement and editorial support of my wife, Jane. She is a master of the art and craft of wordsmithing, and I bow to her in gratitude.

This is the second book she has edited for me, the first being my memoir, Memories, which was written mainly for our kids and a few friends and thus was not formatted for publication. Over time, I identified the theme of my life—overcoming the victim mentality—and rewrote my memoir focusing on this universal message with the hope that it could attract a broader readership.
Jane polished my clumsy efforts.

This book is dedicated to all those along the way who cared.

DISCLAIMER

This is the true story of my life as I remember and experienced it.
Some names and other identifying details of people who played a
role in my story have been changed.

Michael Lewis Moore

CONTENTS

"It is usually quite difficult for the victim to come to see that he or she is living out of the victim identity instead of living from the authentic self, because there is shame attached to their efforts to manipulate and their history of failures. But if he can come to see it clearly and hear the messages it gives him, he can begin to recognize that this mask and costume was never real in the first place, and that there is someone within who is strong and capable and on whom he can rely."

From "The Victim Identity" by Andrea Mathews, LPC, LLC
https://www.psychologytoday.com/us/blog/traversing-the-inner-terrain/201102/the-victim-identity
Used by permission

I cannot over-emphasize how accurately this describes the experience I lived.

Michael Lewis Moore

CHAPTER 1

YOU EITHER JOKE OR DIE, PUNK

Tommy's Drive-In was busy. Though the crowd was light, teens savoring the last night of summer vacation occupied most of the seats at the chrome-framed tables. Hazel Woods, a Black woman almost old enough to be our mother, wiped down the long serving counter. Owner Tommy Lombardo was working on tomorrow's potatoes.

It was late summer 1961 and school started the next day.

Sipping Cokes, Alford Smallwood and I batted the breeze with various friends. After a while, another friend, Bill Robbins, walked in and sat down across from me. "Mike Moore! Where the heck you been all summer, boy?

I smiled.

"South Texas, roughnecking."

He grinned knowingly.

I continued. "Yeah, I just got back in town a few days ago. Your brother-in-law Butch dumped me in a stranger's trailer and left me. Alford showed up and pulled my ragged butt out of that hole this morning. I'm living with his family while we finish high school."

Bill knew why.

"Yeah, I remember you guys raised a lot of hell and skipped too many classes when you were sophomores. Y'all were running wild like a bunch of jackasses. Remember, I was along on some of those runs."

He loved bragging on himself.

"Alford skipped too many classes. I skipped too many semesters."

"I reckon you had your reasons." He drummed his fingers on the table and looked away, remembering.

He was cutting me some slack. I mumbled. "That's passed now."

Bill responded in his twang, "Well, it sure sounds like you've had a helluva day, Mikey. That's kinda like goin' from rags to riches. Good fer you. You were due."

He exaggerated about the riches, but I didn't argue. He took a draw on his Coke, looked me in the eye and grinned like a proud possum with a surprise.

Here it comes.

"I got news for you, son; it was me that told Alford where to find you."

I jolted. He chuckled. Gloating. "Yep, I saw him right here just last night. Your crazy brother told me where he left you. I meant to try to find you, but I saw Alford and told him everything."

Proud now, he leaned back. Bill had just finished doing that which he loved the most: stealing other people's thunder and laughing about it, with faked superiority. I loved him for it. He did it so well he drove some people to madness.

He raised the volume. "I'm glad it worked out for you, Mikey. I figured Alford could help you better than me. I got my own troubles at home. You know that."

With that line, he made himself the hero, and then looked around to see if anyone else noticed.

I nodded in silent acknowledgment.

Friends! God bless them! Why did I want to cry every time someone was kind to me? I swallowed.

We chatted on, mostly about the coming school year. Bill, two years younger than I, attended a different high school. My crazy brother was married to his crazy step-sister.

Alford, two tables away, caught my eye and nodded toward the door. Bill rose with me as Elvis crooned "Love Me Tender" from the jukebox.

Bill drawled a Marlon Brando line, puffing his chest: "Okay, Buddy, let's bust outta this here puke hole," proudly grinning again. Rolling my eyes, he and I walked out. Alford hung back.

We should have waited on him. Alford's blue '55 Chevy was just a few steps away when an unfamiliar 1960 grey Chevy abruptly pulled in front of us and slammed to a stop. I stiffened and made eye contact with the driver.

He was a stranger—an ignorant immigrant or out-of-towner.

He leaned arrogantly back in his seat, put the gearshift in neutral, looked right at me with a smirk and said, "Any of you stupid Odessa sonsabitches wanna fight?"

Oh, God! Surely he'd been drinking! Didn't the fool know where he was? Odessa had a rough-guy reputation. It was like walking into a biker club looking for a badass. There were plenty.

I personally was not one. Usually.

But the wild notion of taking out my long pent-up frustrations and anger on a stranger suddenly made sense. Hell, I was almost relieved.

"Yeah. Come on, guy!"

***

Bill's jaw dropped. He rushed back inside to tell Alford and the others. A crowd gathered.

I led us away from Tommy's to the Odessa College campus across the road. Tommy Lombardo had a strict no-fight policy. The college lawn had thick Bermuda grass for softer landings and the auditorium concealed us in its shadows.

I felt a rush of adrenaline. My anger was tinged with gladness. I could finally vent everything on this nut. In the back of my mind I knew I was foolish, but here by dang was a chance to let it all hang out on an idiot I didn't even know.

Perfect.

I planned to get it over with quickly. I charged him, swinging both fists with all the energy I could muster. It didn't work. I flailed and thrashed, but the artful stranger easily deflected my every effort. His defense was flawless.

I paused. He stared, waiting. He was a trained boxer, maybe even a pro.

That ain't fair!

I charged him again. Same thing.

It hit me hard that I had no chance to beat this guy, so I slowed down and tried to figure a way out of this mess. It was not lost on me that he wanted me to wear myself out so he could go on the offensive and beat me senseless. He knew that I was no contest for him.

I'd have to cheat.

I had him backed up to the pavement separating the campus from Tommy's. We were surrounded by a crowd that was now quiet.

I really didn't want to do what I was thinking. It could have serious consequences. I had the fleeting thought to rush him, throw him to the ground with me astraddle his body. Being a boxer, he might not expect that. I might have gotten away with it, but the guy was quick as a snake and moxie. If I failed with that plan he would start his offense quicker. I had to keep him in his defensive strategy, thinking he was tiring me out.

"Kick him!" Screamed a voice inside my head.

He had his fists in front of his face; his arms and elbows protected his mid-section. He weaved and bobbed, waiting.

I drew back my right fist and stepped into him, but it was a fake punch. He went for it, raising his closed fists to deflect my efforts. That is when I kicked him as viciously as I could in his crotch.

He bent him over with both hands cupping his testicles. Turning away and groaning, he began talking in an effort to stall me.

I let him, hoping I had just won. He groaned and moaned and cursed. "Why did you do that? Damn, you shouldn't have done that." I doubt he expected an answer.

He did not seem interested in quitting.

He recovered and I again threw my fake punch maneuver. It worked. I crushed his nuts again with my right foot, as hard as kicking a football.

He doubled over, then walked in circles, cussing, moaning, groaning, and complaining.

Like a tender-hearted fool, I let him recover a second time.

Now he knew I didn't have the killer instinct. The thought fueled him. He came at me again.

Me? I was on a roll, thinking the third time had to be the charm. I repeated steps one and two, and like Pavlov's classically conditioned hound dog hearing a dinner bell, he bought it again.

The voice in my head spoke again: "Definitely over-trained. You're lucky." I told it to shut up.

I made contact with his tortured balls an amazing third time. Had his balls been a football they would have traveled fifty yards. I gave him his victory, and me a way out. "Okay, guy, I quit. You win."

"Like hell you'll quit."

Huh?

He straightened, fully re-energized, with a killer's sneer. He smelled blood. "There's not going to be any quitting in this fight!"

He bull-rushed me, knocking me down. I was shocked and he was no dummy. This dude had street-fighter sense, too.

His impact knocked me on my back, and quick as a rabbit he was astraddle me. He pressed his left hand hard on my upper chest, holding me down. In slow motion I watched his doubled fist pull back to his ear, taking aim at my face. I could do nothing. He had me.

But as I braced for the inevitable, I realized he was no longer there. I was looking up at the vast west Texas starry sky instead.

Alford had yanked him off me, slammed him to the ground, sat on his chest, and with lightning-fast fists pounded the guy's face. There was a loud cheer from the onlookers urging Alford on.

Bill yanked me up and shoved me into his car. As we pulled away, I looked back and saw the unwilling boxer being yanked out of his driver's seat by some other guys. My brother Butch and two of his friends had driven up just as the fight was over and gave the boxer some more of his own medicine. They finally let him leave, but he caught a red light a block away and an empty Lone Star beer bottle smashed him in the face. He had been introduced to Odessa, Texas.

At Bill's house, we examined my bumps and bruises. Bill gave me a cold, wet wash cloth.

"You got out of that mess with just some knots on your head, Mikey. That's dang lucky. I think he was a lot more than anyone knew. You did things right, for a change, but you are deeper in debt to Alford." He chuckled, highly pleased with himself.

I just took a deep breath.

With a rare seriousness for him, Bill wisely appraised me and offered, "Mikey, you aren't wicked enough to be a real fighter. You're much better off being a nice guy. Why don't you practice on that for a while? Quit the fightin'."

"You're right, Bill. I will. Just don't tell anyone. Take me home."

I was deeply humbled and exhausted. My shirt was shredded. I owned a couple more, and that would have to do. I needed sleep. My anger was dissipated, leaving only sheepish embarrassment. I wanted to start all over.

Savior Alford was snoring in our new well-house "apartment" when Bill dropped me off. I was drifting toward sleep when the water well pump cycled on and off, awakening me. Someone inside the house had just flushed. I hoped my bad luck had been flushed with it.

It had been a heck of a day.

The Friday after Thanksgiving, I heard the back screen door of the main house squeak open and click shut.

Alford stood in our doorway.

"There's a dance at the youth center tonight. Mostly the college crowd from the Odessa High side of town. I want to see them. You going with me?"

"You bet," I said, thinking Julie would be there.

It was late-November nippy when we arrived. If Alford was hesitant because he was still a high school kid, he didn't show it. My stomach knotted. I was green with envy with the excited chatter about college life. I wanted college, too.

We walked in and I hung back, listening and looking. Julie was with a circle of her friends. She had her back to me.

I looked around the huge room. Oh, God!

There he was, alone with a soda in hand, beside the Wurlitzer juke box, scanning the crowd. The dang boxer!

My heart sank.

I couldn't embarrass Julie. Nor could I tell her about the knuckle-busting fight with the idiot by the juke box. I was trying to be good.

I approached the boxer, assuming he knew who I was. "Hey, I want you to know I hold no hard feelings." He didn't recognize me or see my hand, but I could tell his gears were turning.

And then it hit him. He stepped backwards. Did I see fear? He blinked and mumbled something and then left in a hurry, striding past me and out the front door into the cold. I guess he felt like a loser.

When we met, he was an aggressive, pit-bull-like fighter. Now he was meek and mild. I wondered if aggression was linked to testicular health. Or maybe he and Jesus had a good talk about the Golden Rule. Who knows?

Problem solved. No one at the dance saw or heard that quick exchange. I headed to Julie.

Still in love, I tapped on her shoulder. She spun around, surprised.

"Well, hello, Mr. Moore. It's been a while. You're almost a stranger." I saw amazement in her eyes, but she quickly recovered.

"I've forgotten how to dance." I said. "Will you help me remember?" I offered my hand.

Smiling, she put her hand in mine and we moved toward the dance floor. My heart thumped. I hadn't held her hand for years. It was almost surreal.

We danced off and on to slow dances most of the night, for the first time in over four years. During fast dances, I gave her a break. I didn't know how to do the twist.

I didn't mention our shared year of teen-age bliss. Nor did I mention why I broke up with her so cruelly. I wasn't ready to try to explain the muck in my life. I wanted her to know I wanted to be the one she thought I could be. Considering the circumstances I was in at the time, I thought I would have no credibility. We talked about her new life as a college student instead.

She was friendly but noticeably suspicious of my attempted charms. I knew she was confused, but I willed her to sense how deeply I still cared for her.

***

Finally, near closing time, her boyfriend, two years her senior and a junior at Baylor University, appeared at the front door. She beamed when she saw him.

The contrast was not lost on me. Here he was, blazing through college, and here I was, someone who had behaved like a dolt and who was struggling just to finish high school.

My stomach took a dive to the bottom of my emotional pits. I wasn't even close to first place in the race for her affections.

I wanted to go home. What I felt was more than mere tiredness.

I made my way to the exit, passing her boyfriend. He never saw me. His eyes were glued to Julie. Like the boxer before me, I felt like a loser.

I never told her the most important thing of all, that in the years after our break-up, images, mostly of her, pulled me through multiple hellish nightmares. Her sculpting of me was what and who I wanted to be, but she never knew it. I was too conflicted to tell her.

Still, I couldn't quell my feelings for her. Walking alone to Alford's car, I heard that sarcastic voice within me offer words from the Drifters' '50s hit: "Oh, darling, save the last dance for me." My self-mocking subconscious could be such a smartass. The voice knew Julie was saving the last dance for the other guy.

I shivered. The smartass inside shot back, "You either joke or you die, punk."

I breathed deeply of the cold night air and vowed to campaign for a rematch. It would have to be the coming summer. After all, Julie was a freshman at a college three hundred and twenty-one long miles away. I was sleeping in a well-house in Odessa trying to finish high school.

Things can change instantly. That much, I knew too well.

CHAPTER 2

FROM THE BEGINNING

Many have noted that "beginnings are shadowy." My family's beginnings are no exception.

Before he graduated from high school, Allen James "Blackie" Moore, my father, was told by his father to leave home. The reasons have never been clear to me and it was never a subject my father discussed.

He left Wink, Texas, and was taken in by a businessman who owned and operated a billiard parlor on the main street of Grandfalls, forty-one miles away. In exchange for helping run the business after school, Dad was allowed to sleep on a snooker table at night.

I have both of my parents' high school yearbooks from 1938-39. Mom—Lillian Parker—was a sophomore, and Allen James Moore (sometimes called A.J. and sometimes "Blackie" because of his dark, wavy hair), was a junior. Mom was elected Sophomore Favorite that year and was a member of the pep squad.

Nearly everyone who signed my mother's yearbook had kind things to say: "Sunny, Hollywood bound, the best of the sophomores, the biggest flirt in the school, the wittiest, one of the best friends ever, a very intelligent girl" and more in the same vein. Few would argue that she was one of the prettiest girls in the school.

My mother's friends torched my father in his yearbook. They knew my dad had ratted around on her and got caught. Her closest friend chastised him for two-timing her. Another wrote acidly, "I hope you will not always be like you are now."

When Mom signed Dad's yearbook, she wrote: "Listen you Skunk, I think you are about the two-timingest rat that ever walked on two legs. You are the scum of the earth, a low, sneaking, vile, creature, but you are more fun than any boy I've ever seen. May you always keep that sunny smile and cute disposition, Loads of Love, Lillian."

Dad responded as though he was poking his finger at her, accusing her of the same thing: "Dearest Lillian, as you wrote to me, I think you are the two-crossing-double timing little vamp that I have ever seen. (Tell me about it) All jokes aside, Lillian, you are the swellest little girl on this side of heaven. You have a sweet disposition (Oh Yeah). Until you change from all of those, I'll still be, Yours, Blackie Allen Moore (and I am not a preacher)."

I don't know the circumstances of how Lillian and Blackie got married and started a family. Mom was a junior and Dad was a senior. The mystery suggests a couple of options: either they got married voluntarily, or mom got pregnant, leading to a shotgun wedding. In either case, both quit school.

****

I would bet on pregnancy. My mother was seventeen when their first-born, Lindley Allen, known as Butch, arrived in December 1941. Dad was twenty. The rest of us arrived in quick succession: March 1943, April 1944, and October 1945. At the age of twenty-one, my mother had four children under the age of four: Butch, Mike, Shirley, and Lea.

My earliest years were spent in the company of my mother's parents, the Stewarts, not with my mother and dad and older brother Butch. I can only speculate on the reason why.

Possibly my mother was overwhelmed with two toddlers and another baby on the way. Or, it might be that my dad did not want me around.

Like many young men of the era, Dad went away to war, but oddly enough he left behind a pregnant wife, two sons, and a draft-deferred oil field job. If dad left his pregnant wife and two kids voluntarily to fight in a war, then there surely was trouble early in their marriage.

My father had a brother named Lewis, which is my middle name. Lillian and Blackie might have had Lewis in their lives in the early part of their romance and marriage. Lewis was the youngest son of three, and unlike my father, he was allowed to stay at home in Wink until he graduated from high school, after which he volunteered for the Army Air Force. He fought, flew, and died over Libya as the commander of a B-26 light bomber.

My earliest childhood memory is of riding on Grandfather Stewart's broad shoulders, hanging onto his forehead with both hands. There was a sea of excited people around us.

It was dusk and getting darker fast in a crowd of chattering people waiting at the train depot in old downtown Monahans, Texas. The depot was crammed with families and wide-eyed kids as a steam-driven locomotive screeched to a halt. The

Allen James Moore (Blackie)

train was loaded with war equipment and anxious young troops returning home, including my dad.

That memory ends and fades into another scene with a very young me sitting in the back seat of a sedan carrying us through Odessa. To my right was my brother Butch, and next to him was my little sister, Shirley. My dad was driving, and next to him my young mother cradled baby Lea. It was the first time I had an inkling that I belonged to this group. In all my previous disjointed memories I am with my grandparents in their isolated home in the oil patch outside Grandfalls. The Odessa scene was an awakening for me. Memories after these two come more rapidly and more coherently. My brain's wiring was spreading.

After Dad came home from the war in 1946, the whole family moved into a two-bedroom house on an unpaved street in the oil-boom town of Odessa. The house was an asbestos-shingled, two-bedroom, shotgun-type house built for returning veterans and their families. There were others just like ours on the same street.

The local newspaper was delivered by a young man galloping on a palomino. I wanted that horse. The white-uniformed milkman religiously left a sweaty quart bottle of Borden's milk on our doorstep each morning. We four kids slept in the second bedroom crammed with beds. I have no negative feelings or impressions from those early days.

I was hugely impressed when we saw my mom chasing down a stray chicken in our backyard. With wildly flapping wings and terrified squawking, it met its end when she caught it and wrung its neck. We watched in horrified disbelief. That was the kindest thing she did to that chicken the entire day. It was served with delicious cream gravy that evening.

***

East Thirteenth Street was eventually paved and I could see for a mile or more down the gently sloping incline across town.

Dwight Debolt lived near us. He was my very first best friend. His home was exactly one block away from ours. The favorite way for us four- and five-year-olds and our dogs to get to each other's houses was via the dusty caliche alleyway behind our houses, where people kept their trash cans. When we ended that block's long eastward trek afoot, Dwight's home was right across the street, a new, white stucco house.

I never saw his parents at home, but Dwight's older brother Marvin supposedly looked after him, which meant Dwight was as free as the wind. Marvin was Dwight's hero because Marvin was much older and was allowed to do all the things big kids do. Dwight assumed he could do anything his big brother could do. He was my cocky leader even though he was one year younger.

We got our magical tricycles at the same time. Mine was not the horse I wanted, but it was a start. Dwight saw his tricycle as permission to go wherever he wanted, and the paved streets nearby became his highways.

I was riding my trike one day up and down the sidewalk in front of our house when I spotted Dwight coming at me like a demon down the gently sloping street. His elbows pointed out, body hunched forward, and his legs churned desperately like a rider in the tricycle Olympics. He came to a sudden stop, right in front of our home, grinning.

"Come on, Mike, follow me!"

"Follow you where?"

"To the high school." He nodded to Odessa High School at the end of the street.

"What's that?"

Exasperated, he grimaced. "Where *big kids* go to school."

It was so far away that I had never given it any thought, but my smart best friend knew things. I was jealous.

Emboldened by his confidence, I mounted up. We zoomed off, staying on the edge of the pavement, being nice to the cars that would eventually pass slowly by us. Drivers stared, looking concerned, but they were no doubt astonished at our bravery.

 It was gently downhill at first, easier and faster than I had ever gone. I was surely getting more grown up by the minute. We slid to a stop at the busy main street.

Grant Street had a traffic light, which Dwight took as a signal that he had the right of way, being a kid, after all.

Cars skidded to a halt as Dwight raced across the intersection like a demon. I smelled hot tire rubber. Dwight never looked left or right, but he made it! This did not look right to me, but I needed to cross so I pedaled a few feet away from the curb, watching and waiting for a cleared path, hunched over.

A woman in a car to my left came to a stop, opened her door and got out, then turned around and put up her right hand like a traffic cop in downtown Odessa during the Fourth of July, directing traffic just for us. She was so nice.

Grownups just love brave little boys.

To my right, another car had also screeched to a stop, backing up traffic. The driver's left arm protruded out his window, frantically waving up and down, warning cars behind him.

All for us! Wow! But why did they look surprised and scared?

I kept chugging, focused entirely on Dwight. He had dismounted at the curb and had one hand on the handle bars of his tricycle. He was so cool. He cheered me on. "Go Mike! Hurry up! Come on! You can do it!"

I made it!

Off we went when a familiar, early '40s Ford sedan, lurched to a stop, blocking our path.

Mom flew out, slamming her door, her face tomato red and her green eyes blazing. I was instantly crushed; I'd never seen her so upset. I'd been bad, not brave.

"You two wise guys, get off those damn trikes, now!" She roared.

I was awash in shame. Dwight looked insulted that someone else's mom would talk so mean to him, but he complied.

Mom stomped to the passenger side of the sedan, yanked open the back door, and stood like a valet with fire in her eyes. "You two get your butts in this back seat, *now*!"

I did what she said, hanging my head and sniveling. Dwight crawled in looking like a five-star general insulted by the president of the United States.

Mom threw the tricycles like junk into the trunk, then took us home.

She had never yelled at me like that. When we got home, she marched me into the house and sat me down in a kitchen chair. "Mike, what you just did was very dangerous. A car could have hit you and hurt you badly. Don't ever leave this house without telling me first, okay?"

She took a deep breath and glanced away, calmer now. Then she looked at me without saying anything for what seemed like a long time.

"Mike, don't you ever tell anyone—especially your dad—about this. It's our secret. Okay?"

I nodded.

She pulled me against her warm stomach and soft, cotton dress like she was protecting me. I thought the hug was longer than any before.

It hit me hard that every thought I had about brave little boys was wrong. What would happen if I told my dad? It must be bad.

***

My dad ran a Shell service station franchise at one of Odessa's main intersections. When I was six, he saw an opportunity in the booming oil fields in Notrees, Texas, twenty-five miles west of Odessa, and opened his own Shell service station there.

At that time, Notrees consisted of one paved highway with no stop signs or speed limits. There were three service stations, the Caprock Café, Chambers' Grocery Store, a pool hall, a post office, Marvin's Barber Shop and at least eight oilfield camps that provided housing for workers in the oilfields and at the large Shell oil refinery about half a mile across the highway from our home. Two residential neighborhoods were clustered close by.

My parents leased a house behind my father's service station. The Shell refinery pulsed thunderously night and day. Flaring gas torches made the night sky orange.

We didn't have our furniture our first night there, so we slept on the linoleum floor of the living room. We were all abruptly awakened by violent animal noises a few feet away. Lights came on to reveal our cat, Pussy, slashing a bloodied, cornered rat with her sharp claws and teeth. My dad, clad only in his Army-issued boxer shorts, picked up the rat by its long, ugly tail and threw it outside, food for the coyotes, buzzards, and red ants.

I was bewildered by the sudden move, and the cat's fight with the rat did not help. Neither did the events of the coming days.

Within days, without any word of explanation, I was put on a school bus with my older brother and shipped off to Odessa, twenty-five long miles away, to go to first grade.

I knew no one on the bus except my brother, and he sat with someone else. I had no idea what awaited me, and no idea of why was I being taken away from our new home. I was confused and overwhelmed when we pulled up to the old, dark brick elementary school. An adult herded me and the others into a dungeon-like classroom. The teacher looked like the Wicked Witch of the West and she clearly hated us all.

I was brooding in my seat at the very back of the room when all the other students rose from their desks, lined up and left. I just sat there, sick at my stomach, wanting to go home to my momma.

The witch dismounted from her broom, yanked me up from my desk and hissed something vile in my face. I ignored her, for in my mind I wasn't even there. Then she slapped my face, hard. Dumb-ass me, I thought it was just normal to have a teacher slap the crap out of a bad student, which I obviously was.

I had thought that the teacher and I were the only two in the room, but evidently one of the other first-graders from Notrees saw what happened. Gossip in Notrees traveled at hypersonic speed and my mother found me in my new bedroom, got down on her knees and at eye level said, "Honey, did the teacher slap your face when you were at school yesterday?"

I responded with an innocent "Uh huh." With a grim look on her face, she got up and marched out.

I never saw that teacher again, and life was a blur for a few more days until our new grade school, a mile away from our house in Notrees, was finished and ready for occupancy.

The minute our first grade bunch was seated and quiet, Mrs. Miller, a kind, middle-aged woman, asked those who could read to raise their hands.

Nearly a third of the first graders raised their hands. I was shocked and embarrassed. But I was not alone, and that helped my fear.

Mrs. Miller said, "Okay, we are going to work on that, starting right now."

She wrote the alphabet on the new blackboard letter by letter, mouthing the sound each letter made.

I doubt I ever paid more attention to an adult than I did at that moment. I couldn't wait for class the next morning, thinking it would be the day I could read, too. This school was not a dungeon and my teacher was not a witch.

***

Business boomed and my dad bought his first tank truck, which he named Lulu Belle. The next tank truck was bigger, with a powerful pump for killing new wells. The fleet grew. Dad's employees hauled oil and water, killed wells, and cleaned oil storage tanks. Mom was his administrative support.

The service station became a full-time maintenance base and an office was added to our house. Our family car was a brand new 1950 Oldsmobile, possibly the only Oldsmobile in Notrees.

New, wagon-wheel living room furniture filled the family room and Dad added a separate eating area off the kitchen. Two-way radios were installed in the office and in Dad's car. He courted his centers of influence constantly, the old-fashioned way, with good whiskey at the end of a hard day.

Everyone knew everyone.

Notrees sits in the wide-open spaces of West Texas. For the most part, it was a flat sea of scrub mesquite trees and mesquite grass under a dome of infinite blue skies. It was loaded with jackrabbits, cottontails, rattlesnakes, prairie racer snakes, king snakes, and prairie dog towns.

Ancient Native American camping sites and flint artifacts were everywhere. All that space was laced together by caliche roads leading to remote ranches or windmills. Windmills with reservoir tanks were everywhere. They were our private swimming pools in the summer and an oasis for cattle and horses.

We first explored the vast landscape on foot, then on bicycles and in cars, initially thanks to early driving permits.

It was heaven.

****

Things were different at home. I became aware of my parents' marital ills on Christmas Eve when I was in the first grade and Butch was in third grade.

Around eleven p.m., Mom shook us both awake, crying. She closed our door and whispered so our younger sisters couldn't hear.

"Boys, your dad won't come home so I need your help to get ready for Christmas morning," she said.

My stomach knotted. *Where was Santa?*

 "Where is he?" Butch asked.

"Down at the pool hall, playing cards and drinking. I don't know what else to do. I'm sorry, but I can't let him spoil it for everybody—I don't want the girls to know."

Butch was mechanically gifted and went to work with wrenches and screwdrivers to put together toy wagons and doll beds.

I helped with the wrapping and name tags. Shortly after midnight, our living room was fully staged.

We were proud of ourselves, but what about Dad?

Mom tearfully hugged us. I went to bed knowing that I had to help make sure that our two little sisters didn't find out that Santa was a cheap phony. And as I tried to sleep, I wrestled with the question of why my father was not at home on the most important night of the year.

The next morning, Dad was up and smiling, although a bit bleary-eyed. He and Mom made little eye contact or conversation.

As our wide-eyed sisters raced to the tree, Mom turned to Butch and me and winked.

CHAPTER 3

NOT JUST "NO" BUT "HELL, NO!"

The day before my eighth birthday, when Mom asked me how I wanted to celebrate, I said that I wanted to take Diane Brown to eat Mexican food in Odessa, and go to a picture show. I had thought about it for days.

The next night, my family and I, freshly bathed and dressed up, loaded up in the Oldsmobile and drove to Diane's two-story house just down the highway. I marched onto the porch and knocked on the door. Diane's older sister, La Nita, opened the door and welcomed me inside.

She charged back to Diane's room, leaving me standing just inside the front door. Diane's mom and her two sisters were helping her get ready for her first date. I was impressed!

Diane's father was seated across the living room. One leg was crossed over the other and he was smoking an unfiltered cigarette. He nodded at me with a slight smile, but it was not a smile meant for me. I knew that. He took a deep breath and half shook his head as he exhaled a puff of smoke. His expression told me he was amused at the energy his females were expending over Diane's first "date."

Diane emerged, head held high in youthful sophistication. Her mother and two sisters followed her into the front room to watch her leave with Mike Moore. Diane and I, hand in hand, bounded down the front steps.

We ate with my family at a Mexican food restaurant and then watched a movie about the Three Musketeers. Diane and I held hands in the crowded back seat of the darkened car on the way home. My first date was a resounding success.

The experience burned itself into my mind. When Diane stepped into her living room, I experienced an epiphany: All of Diane's family made this a happy time for her. That would never happen in our home. We aren't that close and caring. We don't know how to love. Our dad doesn't know how to be happy.

Not long after, Mom and Dad were in the kitchen talking. She was working at the stove as he sipped a glass filled with amber liquid. I was reading a comic book, not paying much attention, when Dad exploded. "You what? I guess you're trying to be the Mrs. Astor of Notrees, right?" Mom had been shopping in Odessa that afternoon and had evidently bought something that Dad objected to.

She snapped back. "You accuse me? Here you are running around the oil patch in a brand new Chevrolet with a two-way radio barking orders for me and your employees? Plus, you just bought the most expensive Oldsmobile in town! I guess you're Mr. Astor, too, right?"

"You go to hell," he said as he stomped out.

It was the first time they had argued in front of us kids. We ran to our rooms to get out of the crossfire. Even our collie hung her head. I read about the Astors in the encyclopedia in the school library the next day.

***

The dam was breached. From then on, my parents waged open warfare in front of their kids. I liked it better when it was hidden or when others were around. The happy faces came out for company, and especially for longtime friends.

The Van Brunts were my parents' best friends.

Willard Van Brunt had been a fighter pilot in World War II, which fascinated me to no end. He worked for Shell Oil in the Permian Basin centered around Notrees when we were there, but in 1952 he was called up as a Reservist to serve in the Korean War. Based at Goodfellow Air Force Base in San Angelo, he became a flight instructor in the new jet trainers.

One night our old time party-line crank telephone rang our signal, three longs and a short. My dad answered. "Yeah? … Willard! … Okay! …. We'll be there, and thanks for the call! I'll spread the word!"

He hung up and excitedly announced, "Van Brunt will buzz Notrees at noon tomorrow! Lillian, why don't you pick up the kids from school at lunch and we'll all meet at the Caprock Café. I want us all to see this."

I was excited because my parents were excited. Besides, we were going to eat at a café rather than take a sack lunch to school.

It was the height of the lunch hour at the Caprock Café that day when we heard a sound like a gigantic explosion. All the loud chatter suddenly turned into dead silence. The faces of the crowd of oilfield workers reflected dread and horror, thinking of the gasoline refinery a half mile away.

Not me. I sat on a bar stool as close to the front door as I could get. I yelled out, "It's Van Brunt, it's Van Brunt!" In one long step I shot out the door. Shocked adults, dropping silverware and with mouths full of food, chased after me to see what it was that scared the hell out of them and caused young Mike Moore to be so excited.

And there he was, Willard Van Brunt climbing steeply into the blue winter sky and doing aileron rolls. He was in a shiny, new Air Force jet, a Lockheed T-33 Thunderbird that most of us had never seen before. It was Notrees' first airshow, done in style.

With eyes glued to the sky, the amazed crowd watched as the airplane hooked around at the top of a climb and started a steep dive back toward the café, like a strafing run. It leveled off a mile away, right over the highway in front of us. The jet seemed silent in its rush toward us.

It approached at a dizzying speed, and a strange buzzing sound preceded it, a sound made by trillions of molecules being rapidly compressed and pushed out ahead of the jet's path. Then there was another brief silence before the jet's whooshing roar hit us with the delayed sound of jet exhaust. When the airplane blasted by us, it was so low that we could see the two helmeted pilots and the oxygen masks that covered most of their faces.

Both pilots seemingly looked us right in the eyeball. The sleek jet couldn't have been more than a hundred feet above ground when it pulled up into another steep climb and again executed more aileron rolls. It topped out high in the sky, leaving us engulfed in the delayed roar of jet exhaust and the smell of spent jet fuel.

It commenced another diving turn and came right down main street again, barely telephone-pole high, giving us one last thrill. We knew the show was over by the way the jet climbed, without rolling.

I couldn't take my eyes off the airplane as it shrank to a speck in the sky. Finally, and without my brain's permission, my eyes blinked, and the jet disappeared into the distance.

It was all over in a few minutes, but it was the talk of the town for years, and it instilled in nine-year-old me a passion that never died. I wanted to fly like Willard Van Brunt. I was bitten by the bug that bites only a few.

***

My father sponsored a summer baseball team, the A.J. Moore Tankers, that my brother Butch played on the summer before he was a seventh grader. They were good, and they won a championship competing against the best in Odessa, despite not having an official coach. The trophy they won was the only such trophy ever displayed in the trophy case at the Notrees Elementary School. Dad semi-managed the team and we spent a lot of time traveling to nearby towns and at the local ballpark for practices and games. I assumed my turn would come.

In the spring of my fifth-grade year, a new family moved into town. With the school principal's permission, the father, Dean Burleson, organized a fifth- and sixth-grade Notrees track team to compete in the Ector County school programs in Odessa.

He coached in his spare time, without pay, simply because he loved kids' sports. After training with him, my classmates and I competed in Odessa against all the other schools at a huge track meet. We didn't have great athletes, and we won nothing, but it was great experience.

I was a football nut and year-round would throw the ball or play touch football with anyone who was willing. Mr. Burleson called me aside one day and told me he was thinking about starting a football team with me as a quarterback. It was a dream come true. I knew with his help, I could do it. I was pumped.

He came to our house one night to talk to my dad. My mom ushered him into the living room, where my dad sat reading the newspaper. Dad never rose from his chair. Mr. Burleson introduced himself and explained why he was there.

Dad nodded and didn't say anything. Mr. Burleson beckoned to me and placed my hand flat on top of his.

"Look at the size of this hand," he said. "All good quarterbacks have big hands."

I beamed.

"Mike can really throw a football, and has a strong arm for someone his age. He's probably the best athlete in his grade."

My dad sat very still, stone-faced.

Mr. Burleson continued. "I know you sponsored a championship baseball team and I was wondering if you would sponsor a football team?"

My dad finally spoke. "Bullshit."

In a voice dripping with contempt, he went on.

"I seriously doubt you know anything about coaching or talent or even what it costs to outfit a football team. Notrees doesn't need a kids' football program. My answer is 'hell, no'." Then he turned his head, dismissing the humiliated coach. Ashen faced, Coach Burleson said nothing and let himself out.

I was numbed to the bone. Shattered.

My dad angrily picked up his newspaper and hid behind it. He didn't look at me or offer to explain. I walked past the kitchen where mother was washing the dishes. She had to have overheard, but didn't say a word.

I lay down on my bed, the lower bunkbed, which now felt like a lonely, unlit cave. I never felt so disconnected from my family. What the heck was going on in my dad's mind?

The only answer I could fathom was that the man I called Dad didn't like me at all. Why?

Neither one of my folks talked to me about that night, nor I did I ask. I think I was too afraid of their answers.

I couldn't understand why I could be so well accepted outside my home, yet be rejected by my own father. Heck, in the third grade, I was the teacher's pet. What did she see when she looked at me, and what did my dad see that was so different?

***

When Dad's business grew to the point that he needed a full-time mechanic, his ad was answered by a man named Cole from De Leon. I had no idea where De Leon was, but I liked seeing other places, and I asked my dad if I could tag along on the trip to interview him. When we arrived at their new, clean trailer five hours later, a nice, clean cut man met us and introduced himself and his wife and daughter to us.

Cole was one of those guys who would smile and shake the hand of a boy like me and make him feel good about himself, but what I remember the most was his drop-dead beautiful wife and daughter Gayle, who was my age. She had bright, diamond-blue eyes and thick, wavy blonde hair, just like her mom.

The interview concluded with handshakes and promises to see one another soon, and as my dad and I headed home in our new, blue and white 1953 Rocket 98 Oldsmobile four-door sedan, I hoped I could please him and heal some wounds.

Suddenly a beautiful new car came toward us—a brand new 1954 Oldsmobile Rocket 98 convertible with the white top down and with white leather interior and a rich, two-tone paint job. It was far more spectacular than any other car I had ever seen. Even my dad said, "Wow! Will you look at that?"

Even I, a hick from the sticks, sensed that much more was to come and life was to going be exciting. The cars were changing to reflect that.

***

Several weeks later, at the end of my sixth-grade year, Cole and his wife and daughter arrived in Notrees. They parked their house trailer on my dad's trucking yard and my parents helped them get settled in. I again got to search those beautiful blue eyes that would lock onto to mine for an instant and thrill me with an accompanying smile.

Notrees never looked so good. My two sisters befriended their new neighbor and she was often in our home. One day when there were no sisters or adults in evidence, Gayle and I chatted just outside the back door. Gayle made me feel mature because of her cool demeanor.

She paused as though deep in thought and then looked me straight in the eye. She tilted her head slightly. "Mike, do you know how to kiss?"

I could not lie, and I didn't know where this was going. I was sitting on Princess's dog house and my feet stopped swinging. My face turned red.

The best I could come up with was a dubious, "I don't . . . really . . . think . . . so."

"Then I want to teach you." I slipped off the dog house, reporting for my lesson.

"Let's go over there." She took my hand and in a few steps we were behind my house where no one would see us. Very tenderly she embraced me, leaning into me. "Just pay very close attention."

All of my senses were on emergency alert, taking in every nuance of her body language.

She began softly, almost with a whisper: "Let me lead. Don't you hurry. When I change the kiss, you follow. Here, let's try it."

We did. "*Mmm*, nice. Take it slow now, easy, once again."

When we came up for air, she whispered, "You can tell if a girl likes what you are doing. She will move closer to you." Gently taking her right hand upwards she caressed my neck. "Try doing this for me."

"Uh huh." I loved her teaching style. I leaned up against the old green asbestos siding and took my time, treasuring the moment.

Then the screen door opened and slammed shut—my nosy sister Shirley, ruining everything.

I think Gayle must have spent her time gauging when her father was gone and her mother was busy, and I was available. I spent as much time as I could being available.

We completed two prolonged lessons after that, and each time ended with a grateful hug and a pleased smile. My head spun back to normal as I watched her walk away.

But the family didn't stay in Notrees very long, and I don't blame them. If faced with the choice of living in De Leon, Texas, as opposed to Notrees, Texas, I would have chosen De Leon every time, especially if Gayle was there.

When they pulled away and out of my life, Gayle looked back at me as I waved goodbye to my great and beautiful friend.

I often thought about how she made me feel as opposed to how my dad made me feel about myself. There had to be a lesson there.

CHAPTER 4

A GLIMPSE OF THINGS TO COME?

Twenty miles west of Odessa the Caprock rises, slowly building to a mesa about eight miles wide. Passing through Notrees, it then drops off into a strip of sand deposits about 70 miles long and 20 miles wide ranging from Crane County to Andrews County.

The dunes are occasionally punctuated by areas of windswept flat ground between them. In the distance and adjacent to the sand hills, Native American campgrounds are still plentiful under rock overhangs and rock outcrops and are often marked with pictographs, if you know where to look.

The sand hills were our playground, and at the end of the day our footprints left the record of our activities in the sand. The desert is a marketplace for predators, especially at night, and by morning our footprints would be gone, replaced by animal tracks, which are in turn swept clean by the desert breezes, to be reprinted the next night.

When I was in sixth grade, our Boy Scout troop pitched tents and spent two nights on one of the windswept flats, this one within sight of a windmill and cattle watering trough.

Just as we finished our lunch the second day, a noise punctured the profound stillness: a vehicle rumbling toward us from the Kermit Highway, a mile or so away. It drove slowly over the rutted road leading up to the windmill, where it stopped.

Like a curious herd of cattle, in unison we raised our heads and watched, still chewing our Vienna sausages and crackers.

It was a sizeable hay truck, with wooden sides and a gate at the back. The bed was stacked with bales of hay, and sitting on them was a group of girls about our age.

The truck driver, a woman, opened the rear gate and the girls piled out. None we saw ever glanced our way. They were in a world of their own.

Someone in our group gasped, "Holy cow! Look at this!"

To our astonishment, the young ladies stripped down to their underwear, giggling and shouting and racing toward the nearest sand dune.

A helpful voice said, "I have binoculars." We were transfixed.

When the girls gathered back at the truck a little while later, breathless and rosy-cheeked, the driver served them cake and ice cream.

"Wow—ice cream in the middle of the desert?" someone said.

The girls giggled and chatted some more, then sang "Happy Birthday" and got dressed. They loaded into the back of the truck and rumbled back toward town.

Profound silence engulfed us once again.

Even if they had seen us at that distance, they didn't seem to care that we were there, but I never forgot that scene. Maybe it was a message.

***

After six years in Notrees, we spent most of the summer of 1955 looking at houses in Odessa. My parents knew that their growing kids needed to be closer to their many extracurricular activities.

We finally settled on a single-story, ranch-style brick house in a new neighborhood on the rapidly growing east side of town. We moved in August and quickly reunited with many friends and some kin. I was twelve years old.

I was excited to get away from the stinky oil refinery in Notrees, and not having to rise extra early to milked the dang cow we got during our last year there. Odessa always seemed like our real home, anyway.

I will never forget the night before I started seventh grade. Mom and Dad had spent their way into a new world in a grand fashion in a short time. I was lying in my brand new bed in our brand new home, surrounded by brand new furniture. The lights were out but I was much too excited to sleep. The window was open and the cool desert breeze washed over me. I smelled freshly mowed grass, new paint, and new mortar and brick.

My new radio, sitting on a bedside table in front of the window, was turned up just loud enough that I could hear a new group called the Platters singing "The Great Pretender."

The next morning was going to bring a new life with new friends in a new school. I already had one friend—Kathy Brunch, whose family had just moved in across the street. I was as honked as a high-flying goose.

I was a football-crazy youth in a football-crazy town, and I signed up.

A GLIMPSE OF THINGS TO COME?

We practiced on the new Bonham Junior High School fields. It was a heady experience to trot onto that manicured Bermuda grass in a full uniform. The others on the team taught me which girls, athletes, teachers, and coaches were cool and which to avoid. I stayed honked.

And when football season ended, I was introduced to something even more fun: dancing with sweet thangs.

This year of assimilation marked the beginning of the real world of human chemistry, a science not taught in the classroom. It was the chemistry that would shape and direct our lives forever. It would break or swell our hearts, heal our wounds, wither our hopes, or promise heaven. This would be the most important course of all, and we learned it without a word spoken about it.

***

My car-crazy parents bought a succession of cars for my older brother Butch to chauffeur us younger ones around. The first was a Jeep station wagon, but it was traded for a new, ugly but affordable, Nash Rambler. The front seats reclined into a full-sized bed.

I got to tag along when Butch gave some of the older girls in the high school band rides to and from events. Some of them really liked me, and we would smooch in the back seat, along with Butch and his smoocher of the moment in the front seat.

One winter day after school, Butch allowed me to drive the Nash up and down a lonesome rural road, first in one direction and then the other, while he and a band member did some pretty heavy smooching on the fold-down seats in the back. Butch had her bra off and her big—no, huge—pale breasts were in full, eye-popping view.

A football buddy was with me that day, and we had been instructed not to look back or in the rearview mirror. We were to behave while they misbehaved; after all, I was only twelve years old. This was my own personal driver's ed and sex ed class at the same time. We didn't keep our eyes entirely straight ahead.

I was enjoying the driving more than I was enjoying the show in the back seat, even if I didn't have any back support. Finally, the hand chasing match was over. Butch ordered me to pull over and stop. He got out, returned the seats to the upright position, and ordered me and my friend into the back seat while he and the ninth-grade lady got up front. Miss Friendly waved a happy good-bye to us when we dropped her off at her home.

Now I wonder just how many parents thought about their teenagers in that green and white car with the front seats that lay down into a bed. It didn't take my parents long to realize their mistake, and they traded the "bedroom" Nash in on a 1957 Ford Ranchero pickup with no back seat at all. It was totally impractical for carrying four kids around, so it was not long before they traded again.

***

I was excited about entering eighth grade. Sports, cars, and girls became my whole existence.

I spent more time out with my friends than dealing with the tension at home. Sticking around Duane, a football buddy, made for more adventure. Duane was a strong, stocky athlete who bulldozed defenders on the football field. He was smart. He could sing. He was always inventing something or performing physics experiments.

We could be mischievous.

Duane's older sister was in high school, and she dated a lot, which left her new 1955 Ford convertible available for Duane. His liberal parents knew he was a good, safe driver, so they trusted him to use the car in spite of his not being old enough for a driver's license. Duane and I spent a lot of carefree, devil-may-care summer days and nights riding around in that convertible, flirting with young ladies from school.

We drove it to a party given by a seventh-grade cheerleader named Karen. Duane and I arrived with the top down, parked in the middle of the quiet cul-de-sac, cranked up the radio, opened the doors, and waited for the girls to flock to us.

We danced in the street and kissed as many as would let us

.

That was the summer my cousin Don introduced me to Alford Smallwood, who would become my best friend. Athletically built, with beautiful teeth and wavy hair like actor Dean Martin, he was tanned, good looking, an accomplished flirt, and a fun-loving guy from a large, close-knit family. One girl referred to him as Alford the Handsome. Although we lived on opposite sides of town and went to different schools, the bond between us grew strong.

But these good times brought some strange times. My dad was usually the first one up and out the door, tending to his business before any of us kids were awake. But one morning he was there when my sister Shirley, a seventh grader, emerged from her bedroom to head to school.

"What the hell?" he roared.

He ordered her back to her room to dress more conservatively and told her to wash off the make-up, too. We were all shocked.

She was dressed no differently from any other seventh grader at Bonham Junior High. They all wore lipstick and blush and mascara.

Thoughts jumbled in my head. *Every girl in the seventh grade is wearing make-up. Mom thinks it's okay. It's okay with other dads— just not ours. Why are we so different?*

He was not satisfied until Shirley had scrubbed her face clean and exchanged her pink, scoop-necked blouse for one buttoned to the top and covered with a sweater.

His insecurities were beyond my understanding. He had bought us an expensive house in a fancy part of town, but was scared to death when we conformed to the time and place? *What made him so upset?*

Mother drove Shirley and me to school that morning. On the way, she pulled out Shirley's make-up bag and gave her a hand mirror.

"Here," she said. "Just be careful coming home. You can wash it off at school if you have to."

Mother helped Shirley keep this secret from our father and eventually convinced him that the world wouldn't end if his daughter wore a little lipstick and eye shadow.

***

Not long after the make-up outburst, I heard shouting coming from the kitchen.

"You put your family in a nice neighborhood," my mother said, "but we've got the cheapest cars on the street. Why do we have to be poorest-looking bunch on Windsor Drive?"

Very soon, a new 1956 Cadillac replaced Mom's two-year-old Buick Century in the driveway, and Dad replaced his ugly company car with a new, blue and white 1957 Ford.

Butch, who always seemed to be Dad's favorite, brought home some bad grades at mid-term of his sophomore year. Dad pulled him onto the back patio where he screamed and called him names.

Humiliated, Butch broke down in tears. It hurt me to see it.

The next day, Butch had a brand new, 1957 four-door hardtop Chevrolet Bel Air. It was red, and hot. Butch already had the reputation of being able to spin the tires of a wheelbarrow. It was a perfect match.

But what was my dad thinking with these impulsive purchases? I don't believe anyone knew, maybe not even him. The most obvious thing to me was that my father thought enough of my brother to not want to alienate him. I never got that message from him.

I believe that the night of Butch's humiliation by our father, followed by the purchase the very next day of a brand new car for him to drive, marked the beginning of Butch's development as a narcissist.

Any student of the narcissistic personality disorder knows that at its root is a huge inner conflict that asks the question: Am I an idiot, or am I superior? Inconsistent parenting is a huge factor in the development of the disorder.

CHAPTER 5

A VERY GOOD YEAR

Kathy Bunch was our class matchmaker.

She made me aware of girls she knew on the west side, where my cousins Ronnie and Don Moore had lived for some time. I had known about some of these girls already, but as Kathy and I became friends, she made my horizons much broader when it came to the opposite sex.

One day in 1957 I walked out the front door of my house and saw in Kathy's driveway a fancy, brand new station wagon surrounded by a group of giggling girls I had never seen before.

One All-American beauty caught my eye: blonde, medium height, energetic and active with a ponytail swinging. She had a dazzling smile, and was obviously having fun.

Kathy went to the trouble of making the proper contacts on my behalf with that cute blonde, Nancy Leach.

Nancy was the middle child in a loving family that enjoyed one another and treasured laughter and hugs. She had an older sister and a younger brother. She was part of a large crowd of young ladies who went all the way through school together and remained close with one another.

She was a huge inspiration to me because she fascinated me with how happy and fun-loving she was. We were both in our first semester of eighth grade when we started going steady, even though we went to different schools, on opposite sides of town.

We were too young to drive legally or have our own phones, so we were lucky to even meet up at all.

Not being legal drivers was not an absolutely prohibitive situation. Parents of both boys and girls were often liberal when it came to teaching their offspring to drive. Nancy was an early driver, to the glee of her close friends.

I was shocked one day during my lunch hour at Bonham Junior High to see her parents' new station wagon slowly driving through the parking lot.

Nancy and her friends were looking for me. Someone in her car spotted me and squealed, "There he is!"

Nancy honked the horn, and they all waved before heading back across town to Bowie Junior High. That happened several times. I was amazed and humbled that she would do that for me.

Nancy flattered me to no end. She made me feel sky high with confidence and self-worth—emotions I never felt before. I felt lucky to be her boyfriend.

***

On Sunday afternoons, the Ector Theatre was packed with teenagers. The line to the box office stretched down the sidewalk, sometimes down the entire length of the building.

There was a great deal of jockeying as those who arrived late searched for friends closer to the front of the line. This positioning for tickets was important, because it might make the difference in whether or not you got your preferred yeat.

Though many had gone to the movies with their friends since early childhood, now it didn't seem to matter what was showing on the screen. Many were now "going steady," and groups formed, their members searching for the partner they had come to meet. Girls saved seats for the boys, and boys searched for "their" girls the minute they entered the darkened seating area.

The first time I sat with Nancy at the movies was like an out-of-body experience. The place was packed. I knew Nancy would be there, as she and I had agreed beforehand to sit together.

I saw her waving, and with my heart beating faster than usual, made my way through the crowd to her and her friends. I was invited to sit beside her as her girlfriends shifted seats, and I could see it was all pre-planned, which made me feel special and grateful. Little did I know at the time, but I had seen nearly all these girls before.

The feeling of caring that washed over me made me want the movie to never end even before it started.

The lucky ones were settling in, hands finding each other and locking together before resting on skirts puffed up with stiff petticoats. At that moment, it was heaven just to be there.

Soon the lights dimmed, and the noise subsided as the music began, the big red curtains parted, and the screen flickered into life.

Closeness came in increments. Our clasped hands softened a bit as our shoulders touched. We settled comfortably, and then our heads came gently together.
The scent of her hair and the smell of her perfume are etched into my memory for life. Soon, our heads, shoulders, and arms were touching, all the way down to our clenched hands resting on her skirt, an absolutely electrifying contact.

It was pure bliss, and the first time ever I felt exactly that way for someone. Nothing in the years to come quite matched the first-time magic of young love.

It made no difference what movie was showing, because every second was being preserved in my mind, straining and desperately willing the seconds to slow; instead the moments slipped by faster. As the movie played on and the intoxication deepened, our breathing became different, and as our bodies pushed closer together, with a neuro-electrical chemistry signaling that she was feeling the same as I was, I could not stand it. I had to risk it.

We sank deeper into our seats, hoping to become less noticeable, but that didn't really matter, because our faces had come too close to stop now, and besides her hand in mine signaled some way that it was okay, and we began to kiss.

I didn't dare breathe, and the dizzy, dancing way I felt is seared into my memory.

It initiated a lifetime of gratitude.

Inevitably, regrettably, the movie ended. We unclasped our hands, and she brushed all the petticoats of her dress back into shape. We took our time getting to the exit since this was our last chance to hold hands for days. We paused at the door, knowing that on the other side we would find bright sunshine and a long line of cars with mommas at the wheel, looking for their innocent sons and daughters.

My mom drove me home that day. I sat in the front seat, facing away from her, watching the world drift by. Nancy's loving family and upbeat personality proved to me that something was badly missing in our tense household. She had stability; we didn't.

Like the brief slice of sunshine I witnessed on the ranch outside of Notrees, this was all-too fleeting and a painful contrast to the darkness that waited at home.

I also knew that plenty of guys were better looking, smarter, funnier, and more mature than I was, and it was only a matter of time until one of them wooed Nancy away.

***

One day, I was chopping weeds in our front yard when Kathy Bunch, the matchmaker, marched across the street from her house, looking determined to get something settled.

"Mike," she said, "there is a girl named Julie Richards and she is very taken with you. I thought you should know."

She stared intently at me, then marched back across the street, leaving me standing there with my hoe, totally confused.

I had no idea what this was about. She was a dear friend, protective like a loving sister. She knew better than anyone else that I was going steady with her good friend Nancy Leach.

I kept pulling weeds.
Then, on a brisk spring Friday night at a sock-hop in the cavernous gym of our junior high school, it happened. I had come alone because I expected Nancy and her friends to show up.

The gymnasium had been transformed into a dimly lit dance floor, outfitted with twisted crepe paper strung from various basketball backboards. Music drifted from the speakers and kept the crowd busy.

Where was Nancy?

I was alone and fidgeting, wanting to look like I was expecting someone, but my hope was fading fast. I started to leave when I saw someone come through the gymnasium doors.

She was alone—petite and cute. She did not attend Bonham Junior High. She had to be from the west side of town. I was instantly attracted to her.

Alarm bells went off inside my brain. This was Julie Richards.

She nervously scanned the room but didn't see me. I walked toward her and was about ten feet away when our eyes met. Her face showed a jolt of recognition and an almost imperceptible look of disbelief, followed by a pleased smile.

I introduced myself and asked her to dance. Neither of us danced with anyone else that evening. When the event was over, she wrote her phone number on a piece of paper, then hugged me good-bye and left.

I don't recall a single subject we discussed. I don't remember talking about anyone we knew in common; we didn't have to. In the year after that night as we became a couple, in a relationship that developed into an I-love-you-deeply status, I cannot remember ever broaching the subject of how we first got together.

I always wanted to know what made her come there that night, alone, to spend the evening dancing with her good friend's steady boyfriend. What was she thinking?

***

I never called Nancy after that. She eventually learned that Julie and I were an item.

I had given Nancy a charm necklace that had the little silver football on it, and she gave it to Julie. When I next saw Nancy, I could see the hurt in her eyes. I wanted to hug her and tell her I loved her. I wanted to be her friend always, but I was too young and dumb.

All I felt for Nancy never changed, even though I deeply fell for Julie. She was an everlasting inspiration for me.

Barely five feet tall, Julie pressed her head against my chest when we danced. She wore glasses and looked intellectual. I learned later that many of her friends thought she might be the smartest in her class. People called her cute; I agreed. I was totally flattered that someone like her would be interested in me.

Her magic was how she made me feel about myself. She made me more confident than I felt I had any right to feel.

We went steady for a full year, from the spring of my eighth grade year to the spring of my ninth. With her, I lived the epitome of teen life in the roaring fifties. She knew many people, and we were invited to many parties.

The first one was in a spacious, graceful home on an aptly named street, Casa Grande, in the nicest part of the west side of town, where long-established oil and insurance families resided. A dimly lit patio served as a dance floor where we danced and talked with Julie's friends.

Best of all was the rear half of the massive back yard, where a peach orchard grew. It was not well lighted, and that is where we walked hand in hand just to be alone. We kissed, and kissed some more, until we decided we'd best return to the party before a search party was organized. It was a sweet summer desert night with a soft breeze.

Families from the west side of town sponsored dances that required white dinner jackets and tuxedo pants. My mother was proud to buy these for me and show me how to put everything together. Julie and her friends wore formal dresses with corsages.

Our parents were living vicariously through us, and I don't blame them. We were having a blast. It was a thrill to pick up my date in our new, red '57 Chevy and drive to the Lincoln Hotel ballroom or Odessa Country Club, where we were ushered into a formal ballroom.

***

My dad's business phone in the den was a reminder that customers often needed to reach him after hours. It was a cardinal sin for us kids to get caught talking to our friends on that line. We had a family phone in the hall outside the girls' bedroom door where someone could sit on the floor and conduct what phone business needed to be conducted, but with the entire family depending on that one phone, it was way too busy for me.

 I turned fourteen around the time Julie snagged me like a big fish. She lived and went to school on the west side of town, and that made the phone important.

I had been quiet about what I wanted for a birthday present; I knew what I was going to ask for, but I had a plan, and I didn't want to act prematurely. I schemed and plotted and waited, hoping my parents would be caught off guard and not remember or say anything about the date.

I wanted to catch them by surprise, at the last moment, hopefully in a moment of guilt for letting the date sneak up on them. I knew my mom never forgot things like that, but our household was busy, with four kids and the family business.

I got lucky.

On the big day, I got up earlier than anyone else, wolfed down my breakfast, and left for school. I got home later than usual. When I came through the front door, Mother and Dad were in the kitchen. Their conversation was muted. I knew why: they had remembered too late that it was my birthday—just as I had hoped.

I casually walked into the kitchen with a somber look on my face. I didn't make eye contact as I scanned the room for evidence of a present. There was none—perfect. I wanted them to think I was disappointed that they forgot me, which in reality I was, but I was also ambushing them, so I felt a wee bit of guilt. But not that much. The victim of their oversight was on his way to being the winner.

Mom hugged me and rather sheepishly wished me a happy birthday.

Dad stood there, a little embarrassed. I just nodded. Guilt filled the kitchen.

Finally, Mom said, "Mike, forgive me. I forgot. We don't have a present. I'm sorry."

I just shrugged, somberly, my clenched fists in my jacket pockets.

Finally, Dad asked what I wanted for my birthday.

I had them! They thought I was a victim, but in reality it was the other way around.

After a long, cheerless pause as I appeared to deliberate, I looked first at one and then the other. Then, with all the calmness I could muster, I said, "I want my own private phone, beside my bed, in my room."

Then I held my breath.

I knew that if they wanted to discuss it, my cause was lost. What I was asking for was unfair. But the other kids in the house weren't on the jury, and under the circumstances, I had my folks by the short hair.

Mother said, "I think that can be done."

I am positive that my dad stood there thinking that this was no time for him to argue, since he had bought my brother a used '53 red Chevrolet convertible just months before. In a few days, I had a beautiful, beige telephone of my own.

***

The school year ended and summer came, as did driving privileges in one of the three family cars in the driveway. (I got my driver's license when I turned fourteen.) There were poolside parties in beautiful homes. There were double dates under the starry skies, and evenings together at the movies, and most of all, there was the feeling of believing that I was one of the luckiest guys in the world.

I cared deeply for Julie, and I suspected she felt the same about me. God was in His heaven and all was right in the world.

The super-intelligent Cameron Ray, who lived around the corner and two houses down, was my "summer friend." He didn't play sports because rheumatic fever had affected his heart, so during the school year, when I was playing football, I didn't see him much. But we had a lot in common.

One day that summer, Cameron ambled around the corner toward our house. I called him over to show him our new, bright red 1953 convertible, which I loved.

"Wow! When did y'all get this one?" He was amazed at how fast the Moores went through cars.

Me, too.

"About a week ago. It's my turn to use it tonight. I'm gonna put up the top and spiff this booger up some. Help me out and we'll cruise the town tonight."

"Ha! You are Tom Sawyer painting a fence, aren't you? But I'm game!" He grinned.

We washed and polished it, put the top down again and snapped the white leather cover over it. We went over every inch of chrome. It gleamed in the summer sun, and it was all ours. Big brother Butch would have to stay home while Cameron and I cruised around town.

Or, so I thought. At the last minute, Butch appeared, wanting to tag along.

Surprised that he would want to join us, I said he could, but reminded him that I would be driving.

What a change!

I never thought I would see the day when he would consent to sit in the back seat. Since I was two grades behind him, it felt odd to have him with us as I called the shots about where we would go. He went with us, but I could tell he resented not being in charge. While Dad probably knew about this turn of events, I didn't care. We had a great time cruising the drive-ins and being seen with the top down on a perfect summer night.

I felt so privileged. By this time, it was obvious that despite knowing a lot of people through the school band, Butch never had a close friend. No one stopped by our house to see him. He could mix well but something—which I later realized was humility—was missing. I think our dad sensed it. I also think he resented me for being the opposite.

***

Because of my friendship with Cameron, his father offered me a part-time job at his service station that summer. The pay was next to nothing, but that was okay; I wanted the experience.

Julie sometimes volunteered to gas up the family car, and she used the opportunity to visit. She always honked the horn as she drove by if she was unable to stop. My schedule was flexible, so I took off when I wanted to do something with her.

It was a good summer that came to a close too soon.

On the Friday of that first week of ninth grade, I was exhausted after a hard football practice and a busy week. Still summer hot, it was dusk and growing darker as I talked with Julie on the phone after supper. I was lying on my bed, fully clothed.

When I was with Julie, or talking with her on the phone, all was right. I felt bold and confident and ultra-appreciative of our relationship. There was a lull in the conversation, and then I said the magic words. I told her I loved her.

I felt her take in a quick breath as though my words had taken her by surprise. For an instant I wondered if I had gone too far and was about to get admonished. I held my breath, and then with a softness and a convincing sincerity, she told me she loved me, too.

Wow! Did life ever get better than this? Is growing up going to be great, or what? I was in such a total state of bliss and relaxation in the pleasant dark confines of my room, with life absolutely perfect, that I drifted into sleep, the phone still on my pillow. It was full daylight on a cool summer morning when I opened my eyes and realized what I had done. It was as though the night had passed in the blink of an eye.

The phone was still next to my ear. I'd not moved throughout the night. It was still early, around seven. Counting the minutes, I waited until nine before I called Julie.

"Julie," I told her. "I'm so embarrassed. I don't know why I fell asleep so fast. I remember everything. It just seemed like I blinked once and suddenly it was daylight."

She was gracious, and laughed about it, "You were extending the moment. I knew that and I appreciated it."

She was an artist when it came to making me feel good about myself. She was the perfect antidote to my father, and I loved her for that.

***

Around that time, I went to Mother and told her the soles of my shoes were worn through and I needed a new pair.

I thought nothing about it, but that night, my father came into my room as I was getting ready to go to a sock hop. I was surprised. I could smell that he had been drinking. He wasn't smiling.

"You don't need a new pair of shoes" he sneered. "Just wait a minute."

He left and returned with a pair of his old shoes. "These will do you just fine," he said. "Put 'em on."

Dumbfounded, I did as I was told. They didn't fit. They had conformed to his feet and were stiff. But I didn't want to challenge him, and just nodded. He spun around and left, not asking or caring if the shoes fit.

They were an old man's worn-out ankle-high shoes, almost as ugly as a brogan and not anything like the penny loafers my classmates wore. Did anyone understand him? I sure didn't.

No kid in my school would have worn those shoes unless under the threat of death, but I felt I couldn't argue. It was like he was daring me to say something.

I went to the sock hop and had no sooner stepped onto the dance floor when a football buddy came over, snickering

 "Where the heck did you get those things?" he said.

I just walked away, but as soon as his back was to me I walked the mile home in the dark, thinking. I realized that my dad would never have forced this humiliation on his older son. I was the only one he treated that way. I went straight to bed and decided I would stick with my own damned, old shoes with holes in them!

The next morning, a Saturday, Mom woke me up and told me to get dressed.

She kept her eye on the clock as I ate breakfast. As the clock hands moved toward nine, I realized she was planning to take me to buy some new shoes. I polished off my eggs and we drove to Dunlap's department store just as it opened. Neither of us said a thing about my dad's old shoes, but the look on her face said it all.

It struck me that there might be a war going on between my mom and dad over me, although I didn't know why.

*****

Outside of my home life, life that fall couldn't have been better. Our football team won every game. I stayed busy with school activities, dances, and best of all, dates with Julie.

Things were perfect when I was with her. Even the weather cooperated: rain fell, breaking a devastating seven-year drought.

My ninth grade year started with excitement and promise. But in hindsight, two events seemed like a portent. I lost the one adult who seemed to care for me unconditionally, my best adult buddy: my Grandfather Stewart, who died suddenly of a heart attack. In addition, my parents' best friend and my hero, the pilot Willard Van Brunt, was killed in a car crash while working in Venezuela for Shell Oil Company.

Still, we lived in one of the most oil-rich regions on earth. The world would always burn gasoline, and Odessa produced gasoline for the world. My dad's business occupied an important niche in that industry. Our future was secure forever.

And then the economy in our area began to collapse. The impossible actually happened.

CHAPTER 6

MELTDOWN AND AFTERMATH

In 1958, the major oil companies operating in the Permian Basin announced that they were shifting their search for oil to the largely untapped supply in the Middle East.

Right before our eyes, the employee camps in Notrees were dismantled and homes were gifted to tenants who wanted to pay to have them moved. All unclaimed houses were demolished. Notrees went from busy burg to near ghost town almost overnight, drying up like a wet sponge in a hot desert wind—as did my father's oil-dependent business.

I suspect the pressure led my father to drink more, though at fourteen I never put the big picture together. I was too busy enjoying the good life, as were my brother and sisters. We were shocked at the terrifying scene we witnessed one night in early November.

It was a school night, and Dad had come home late. We kids were in our rooms finishing homework and getting ready for bed when we heard a crash of glass breaking and our parents shouting at each other.

When we ran to the kitchen, we saw a casserole dish and its contents smashed on the tile floor, evidently thrown there by my father.

My mother was on her hands and knees, and my father pressed his hand on the nape of her neck as he roared, "I said to clean it up, dammit!"

Mom was crying as she yelled back, "Blackie, let me up and stop this!"

With a stricken look on his face, Butch stepped in to help Mother. I had a deep fear of my father and sensed that if I tried to help, I would make things even worse. I went to my room and closed the door, not wanting to see my mom degraded. Numb, I sat on my bed and listened as the commotion subsided.

Our dad was out of control, morphing into a person we didn't know. Suddenly, I feared the future. What would happen next? Where were our lives headed?

The next day passed in a blur. Football season had just ended, and as I walked home from school in the early darkness, it seemed strange not to be practicing for the next football game. As I approached our house, I could see that every light was on and my father's car was not in the driveway.

When I got closer, through the living room windows I saw my brother and two sisters, all sitting on the living room sofa, very erect, wide-eyed, and grim. Mom stood stiffly facing them.

My stomach formed a tight knot as I walked into the brightly lighted room. Mom greeted me with a tight nod. I nodded back, waiting.

"Mike, I want to know how you feel about me divorcing your dad," she said. "Your brother and sisters all agree that it is probably for the best. What do you think?"

Without speaking, I shook my head no and went to my room.

My first thought was that an intact family was better than a broken one, but I had to admit that internally I agreed with her. She was sick of his abuse and terrorizing. She had to change things—to protect herself and her children. The degrading scene the night before was the final straw.

She had evidently spent the day with a lawyer, preparing divorce papers to serve on our alcoholic, out-of-control father. I couldn't stop that train now. I didn't want my mom to think I was not supportive of her, and I understood her reasons, but I had reasons of my own, ones I couldn't say out loud.

I could anticipate what would happen. Butch would appropriate "our" '57 Chevy for himself. Dad would be gone, so I wouldn't have access to his car. Mom would need her own car. And without a car I wouldn't be able to date Julie.

Accepting the situation filled me with anger that I couldn't express, anger that persisted for years even as I worked to understand it. I was mad at my entire family for the dysfunction that defined us and forced me apart from Julie.

I was embarrassed and ashamed. I was fourteen years old and powerless. I reasoned that what I had to endure, Julie would have to endure, and that was not fair to her.

Her family was the polar opposite of ours. Even if she stayed with me, she would eventually be forced to save herself, of that I was sure. To ask for her help in dealing with the trauma I was going through would be like asking her and her family to raise me while my own fell apart. They might pity me, and I hated pity.

I was the only one in our household who really knew what it was to be loved, and they, with their solidarity for the divorce, had stripped that from me.

Damn them all. I was trapped—a victim.

***

Dad was stone-cold sober when he was served with the divorce papers and a restraining order the next evening.

Furious, he charged into the house and twisted Mom's arm upward behind her back, nearly breaking it, cursing the whole time. She screamed, and this time all four of us kids pulled him off of her before he stormed out.

I suspect that Mom called the police, because he went to jail for violating the restraining order. Dad would have been surprised to learn that the law allowed a wife to bar her husband from his own home. I think Dad was one of those people who thought his own morality trumped the law. He would learn otherwise, the hard way, over the next two years.

Utterly depressed, I still had to go to school the next day. My last class of the morning was art. I had had Mrs. Brookins for art for three years, and when I slumped into her classroom she knew something was wrong.

The hour dragged by as I stared out the window. Finally, the bell rang. As the students scattered for lunch, Mrs. Brookins stepped in front of me, blocking the door. Only the two of us were left in the room. "Mike, what's wrong? Are you feeling sick?"

I had bottled up all that I was feeling, and her kind, compassionate presence made me feel vulnerable. Finally, between sobs, I confessed, "My parents are getting a divorce."

There—the words had been spoken. The situation became real and I had just told the whole world.

She put her arm around my back and said gently, "Come on. Let's go to the cafeteria and have some lunch. My treat."

The two of us ate in silence, but it was comforting to just be with an understanding adult. We finished eating, and I thanked her and left. It was a miserable day, and I had decisions to make about how to face my friends. The social life I had known was no more.

***

When Mom told Dad that I had voted against the divorce, he asked her to tell me to meet him downtown, alone. Mom let me drive her car there.

We met in front of the Ector Theatre. As he walked toward me, I thought that he emanated pain. He had dark circles under his eyes, and his shoulders drooped. His was the face of rejection.

I waited, my stomach in knots. At first he was silent, and then he asked, "Is it true that you were against the divorce?"

I nodded.

He stared at me as he considered his response. I think it hurt him to know that I was the only one who wanted to keep the family together. I wondered if he was the most hurt because his two favorites, Butch (of many cars) and Shirley (his adoring princess) had sided against him.

He took off his wedding band and put in my hand. He said, "You keep this. It's yours now."

And without another word, he walked away.

I was shaken. I hurt for him. I hurt for my family. I hurt for me. I had no idea what he expected me to do with that ring, and I never asked him. I kept it in a small box on the top shelf of my bedroom closet, untouched, for years. I never looked at it. I realize now that deep down, I hoped my parents would mend their marriage and he would ask for it back. That request never came.

I was rattled to the bone with how fast our lives had changed. I was too ashamed to share the news with anyone. The worst thing of all was that there was no stability for us kids anymore.

***

Mom's last portrait

Mom took a job as a bookkeeper and worked long hours, and she often had dates in the evening. Thirty-four years old, she was attractive and vivacious; I'm sure she didn't want to spend the rest of her life without a partner.

Our home turned into a teenagers' free-for-all, a mix of anxiety and unlimited freedom.

Within a few weeks, Butch quit high school, got married, and soon was a father. He took the "kids' car" with him, as I knew he would. Embarrassed that their mom was dating, our sisters Shirley and Lea decided to live with our father, who had bought a nice house on the other side of town.

With Mom gone so much, I was often left alone in the big ol' house. I had no transportation except that provided by friends.

For several months, I tried to connect with Julie by phone every day, but it put me under tremendous pressure emotionally to keep the dramatic change in my life from her. She didn't deserve to be dragged through the incredible dysfunction afflicting our family.

Saying it was Sadie Hawkins Day, on our last date Julie picked me up in her family's car. Another couple rode in the back seat. There was no real activity planned, and we drove around and smooched at stop signs in quiet neighborhoods. I always suspected that she instigated the event because I was now without a car, but I didn't ask.

That spring, I broke up with her.

I called her and simply told her I did not want to go steady anymore. I hung up before she could say a word. It made me sick, but I felt I had to shield her from the craziness in my life. What she didn't know was that I loved her even more now that she was no longer my steady girl.

I became depressed. I was functional, but grossly unhappy without her.

I didn't tell her, but I wanted Julie to date others and have a "normal" high school experience that she would not get with me. I clung to the hope that we would make up once I graduated and was on my own.

***

When school started in September, Odessa High School bulged at the seams. The new Permian High School was not yet finished, and the incoming sophomore classes from the two sides of town merged. The friendly interaction made the school year of 1958-59 an electrified high point for both groups. Julie and Nancy's crowds joined the east side crowd, of which I was a part.

But my home life made focusing on class work impossible, and I foundered. I skipped class so often that I passed only two courses, and those just barely.

I was a bad influence on some good guys, talking them into skipping classes and going to places like the drag races in Fort Worth. It was no holds barred for Mike, and it hurt my buddies, too. Alford Smallwood and Cameron Ray raised cane with me but I didn't change a thing in my own life.

After a miserable, lonely Christmas break, I toyed with the idea of quitting school. I felt like a phony, detached from my friends, and with no positive identity, no allowance, no car, and little adult supervision.

The shame was toxic.

***

In early 1959, my mother evidently lobbied my father to buy me a car: a worn-out 1955 Chevrolet, two-door post 210 with a v-8 engine, standard shift and no radio. It had been a company car but it was my favorite color—sky blue—and I fell in love with it.

It took me to a new world.

Cameron and Alford and I installed a higher-performance camshaft and rigged up a race with a friend. The friend won and my engine oil pressure went to zero. A deep knock signaled that engine failure was imminent.

We limped it home, parked it in the garage, and started scheming. I told my mom that the old, worn-out engine had failed, but if she would lobby Dad for a new short block assembly, my friends and I would save money by providing all the labor.

Amazingly, a Corvette engine did not cost much more than a stock engine, so my worn-out '55 Chevy ended up with a hot 1958 Corvette engine. We managed to find deals and trades, and when all the finagling was over, I had two monstrous, four-barreled carburetors and everything to go with them. We lowered it in front, put loud mufflers on it, and stripped off some of the factory chrome to give it a customized look.

It was bad ass.

By this time, I had abandoned sports and school, but was accepted by the guys who loved hot, fast cars. My brother had been one of them, and my car became an escape from reality and my new identity.

I had casually dated a girl named Jackie Brown all summer, and I told her I wanted to quit school. Good-hearted Jackie argued with me— she cared and knew I was not doing the right thing for myself and others, but I insisted.

One evening when Jackie and I were in my car at Tommy's Drive-In, I thought she seemed preoccupied. She constantly surveyed our surroundings, but that was not unusual, as the place was packed and rocking. Suddenly, she opened the passenger door without saying a thing and left, leaving the door wide open. Julie Richards climbed in. Oh, my God.

***

Deadly serious, Julie said, "Mike, Jackie called me. She said you want to quit school. She wanted me to talk to you. You're making a huge mistake."

I was speechless and just stared at her. I could not believe she was actually beside me. Shame washed over me. I was drowning in it. I couldn't tell her a thing so I just nodded stupidly.

In a flash, I knew Jackie knew I still cared for Julie. In another flash, I knew they both cared, and I knew I was abusing them. Nancy cared for me, and I had abused her with my cowardice.

Geez! I always hurt those who cared!

The only solution I could see was to distance myself from them and quit being a phony about my feelings. I didn't know how to do that, but it seemed logical that getting away was my only option.

Julie left and I sat there in stunned silence. Jackie did not return. I couldn't blame her. I drove home to be alone in my big, empty house. I decided to withdraw as much as I could. I never went back to school. Incredibly, I heard nary a word from either parent or any school officials about it.

Alford and Cameron pressed on through the school year not knowing what I was feeling or thinking.   They earned poor grades, but their parents would never allow them to drop out. Ironically, both Alford's mother and Cameron's mother worried about me and told their sons to keep me from getting in trouble.

I thought that was amazing, since I was the bad influence on them, but I also knew that they knew that if I got into deep trouble I might be without parental support. Bless them! Both of those mothers were world-class all their lives.

I was a hermit. While the other kids were in school, I stayed home and read books from our well-stocked shelves. Mom was a Book of the Month Club member, and in addition to best-sellers she had accumulated a thirty-volume set of the collected works of various authors. There were some high-brow authors in that set of red books.

I became an avid reader. It was an escape, of course, and I realized that, and I was okay with it. I read the ones that were interesting, but I just picked through most of them. I devoured the works of H. Ryder Haggard, author of King Solomon's Mines and other wild adventure stories. I didn't care much for Shakespeare. No regrets about that. Charles Dickens kept me busy for a while, but Mark Twain was my favorite.

I couldn't relax at home while alone, and became an insomniac. Sometimes I stayed up all night reading, falling asleep when it started to get light outside. On many nights, after midnight I would get in my car and drive to the other side of town. I slowly drove past Julie's house, staring at her window. I fantasized every single time about hopping over the rock fence and tapping on her window to talk to her, but I was afraid of getting caught and being banished from her presence forever. I would drive home and go back to reading until dawn.

As the weeks passed, I pondered what my future would be like without a formal education. Maybe I could be a businessman and open up a speed shop for high-performance cars and make a good living. But it was a questionable goal. Where would I get the money? The idea didn't make me feel any better.

Those lonely times reinforced something that deeply disturbed me: my parents and my brother never finished high school. No one in my family seemed to be concerned with how this restricted their opportunities.

I started to read about college football in books I checked out from the library. I became aware of college life and how different it was from anything I had ever experienced. From a young age, I knew I didn't want to make a living in the oil business like so many others did, so why did I choose to limit my options? I was as dysfunctional as those around me and it made no sense looking at it through that lens.

The more ambitious kids in my school often talked about college, and that left me with still another knot in my gut as I realized those I admired the most would leave me behind.

I had to change.

***

Quitting school had been a mistake, but it was too late to salvage the school year, so I waited for the new school year to start. Summer was coming, and my friends and I would no doubt be a part of the active car and drive-in scene.

Meanwhile, I languished in reclusive shame at home while my bad-ass car sat in the driveway until a buddy called me to go cruising the town or to Tommy's Drive-In.

One Saturday afternoon that summer, Alford, Cameron, and I were just completing a circuit around Tommy's when Nancy Leach burst out of the door to Tommy's, poked her head in my window, and said, "Hey, I want to drive this hot rod, so scoot over!"

Geez, I loved that girl!

I moved to the middle of the front seat, and she yanked open the driver's door and slid under the wheel. She could drive a standard shift, but had never driven a car with a beefed-up clutch and hot rod engine. We lurched and the engine stopped on her first attempt.

I said, "Nancy, push as hard as you can on the clutch pedal and let it up as slowly as possible."

"Okay, okay!" she retorted. She tightened her jaw and got us onto the main street. She accelerated, but her foot was too heavy on the pedal, and the blue rocket jumped forward with a growl.

"Wow!" she exclaimed. "This thing is awesome!"

Haltingly, she went around the block and back to Tommy's, where her pack of friends waited, all wide-eyed as my hot car's loud exhaust rumbled. Nancy looked me in the eye sweetly and said, "That was fun, Mike. See ya." And then she got back in the car with her lady friends. Nancy had forgiven me for deserting her for Julie.

She was impossible to forget.

She made my day. She also ruined my clutch, so I drove straight to the parts house and bought a new clutch plate and went home and changed it with the help of my buddies. It was going out anyway. I vowed that if she ever wanted to do that again, it would be worth another clutch.

***

When the brand new Permian High School opened in the fall of 1959, I enrolled as a sophomore while my friends started their junior year, with college in sight. The building was state of the art, and the football team was doing fairly well. It all added to an air of excitement that even I could feel, but I stayed withdrawn.

Second only to a Corvette, I did have the hottest car in the parking lot, and that made me acceptable to the car crowd if I so desired. I lived in two different worlds when it came to a social life, but I didn't stand out much in either one, and that was fine.

I worked at the Ray family service station until the spring semester, when I saw that I was spending too much time there for too little pay. Besides that, working until closing time interfered with homework.

Home life was lonesome and I wanted to change that. I thought I could come up with a plan to shape my mother and me into a little, normal family. Maybe if we got rid of the big house and found a smaller, less expensive one it would take pressure off her.
I began prowling both sides of town looking at houses for sale. I loved the old, stable neighborhoods on the west side near my cousins, and found three or four available houses.

I tried to sell her on the idea by saying the yard was too much to handle and the pool was a mess. At first she just stood there taking in what I said, then replied: "I've got some time. Come on. You drive my car."

As I drove I told her, "Mom, let's try to make our lives easier. I'd like to be more of a part of your life. I think there is way too much going on." She pretended to be interested, but was noncommittal. I thought she was considering my suggestion, so I let it simmer.

I drove by three houses for sale, but she never said a word. I took that to mean that she didn't want to leave our house on Windsor, so I glumly accepted that. I didn't want to upset her, because lately she had not been feeling well, staying home for several days at a time. It didn't occur to me that something might be seriously wrong.

Still, I missed her and any semblance of family life. When she felt well, she would leave the house for days at a time. I never asked why, and she didn't explain.

I decided to try to shame her into admitting that I needed a mother in my life. I began translating my frustration into a speech I would give to her, a demand of sorts, or at least an assertive move, and she would have to deal with it. I would play the victim card. I would catch her in some state of guilt.

I confronted her one night when she arrived home after an unexplained absence of several days.
I asked her to sit down and then I stood, as if giving a speech.

"Mom, I want a mother," I said. "I want something of a home life. I don't understand what's going on with you. I'm trying to be loyal to you because you've always been loyal to me and I love you. But this is hard, being here all the time wondering when you'll come home. Can't we do something about this?"

Surely that would touch her.

She said, "Mike, you can do whatever you want with your life. I just want a life of my own." Then she stood and said, "I'm not feeling well," before disappearing into her bedroom.

I was stunned and hurt, but sensed that something else was terribly wrong. I went to the front yard and sat down cross-legged in the summer grass. There was no moon, and I felt protected by the dark. I forced myself to objectively analyze what just happened. This was not the time for the emotion I was feeling. It was the time for a diagnosis of what she said and did. I needed to understand something, and I am sure part of that need was ego protection.

I reasoned that Mom had terminated an abusive relationship because she felt unloved by her husband. That much was obvious. She has to be in grief about the reality of that fact. She is dating, which means she is trying to prove herself loveable and wanted by someone. I could understand that.

The daughters she had protected had abandoned her by living with their father. Butch, her first-born, had left to get married to a woman who did not like her and had denied her access to her only grandchild. Butch did nothing to resolve that situation. That had to hurt. Mom had received and shared with me an anonymous letter that stated things that could only have come from a sick mind. Mom and I agreed that it had to have come from Butch's wife.

Mom must feel completely betrayed.

Maybe she thought that I would jump ship, too. I would never have done that, and I thought she knew it, but maybe I was wrong. Where did I stand with her now?

I still struggled with that question the next day. I knew she was not feeling well because she had slept a lot and hardly left her bedroom. I didn't want to leave her alone, so I stuck around.

I felt that we had been avoiding each other, and it was her turn to talk to me.

Finally, she emerged and asked me to come to her shade-darkened room. She was upset and had been crying.

 "I want to tell you something, Mike," she said. "Dr. Leikish says I have fatal pancreatitis. I'm dying, and I won't last long."

Shocked and speechless, I hugged her tight, but I was stunned and unable to speak.

Could this get any worse? Scared for my future, too, I let her be alone. I again went to the front yard, and again it was dark. I sat in the soft grass with my back to the street and wept.

A car approached and slowed. An old football buddy was on his way home. I hardly moved. Sensing something bad, he asked what was wrong. I told him that my mother was dying.

Rattled, he stood there and finally said in a quiet voice, "I'm sorry, Mike." He got in his car and left me alone in the front yard.

It had been a year of turmoil for the entire family and it was obviously not getting any better. Everything felt lonesome, dark, and lost.

But as I sat there, a hopeful thought came to mind. Maybe she would be okay. She might just need attention—to know that she is loved. Surely a thirty-five-year-old, healthy-looking, pretty woman couldn't die so prematurely.

Wanting to believe that, I dove into a barrel of denial. I told no one, not even my brother or sisters, about Mom's diagnosis. I was determined to face the world as though everything would be fine.

Trust in God, and everything will be all right—that was the favorite saying of most everyone in west Texas. I'd give that a try. After all, nothing else had worked in the last year or two.

CHAPTER 7

THE COLLAPSE OF THE MOORE FAMILY

Early in 1960, while still living with my mother on Windsor Drive, I got a strange call from my father. He and my mom had been divorced for nearly two years, and I had had hardly any contact with him in all that time. But now he demanded that I come to his house, pronto. He sounded angry and I had no idea why.

When I arrived, I saw that my brother, who had a wife and two children at home, was there, too, and I could tell he was also curious about what was going on.

Dad was bulldog-slobbering drunk and mad and evidently wanted someone to take it out on, and he took it out on us. He forced us to strip naked, and we stood like soldiers in review in front of him while he berated us in an incoherent tirade.

"Look at you . . . you think you're such hot shots, and you, Mike, with those stupid pants," he said. "Who do you think you're trying to be?"

I didn't answer him. Then came the bomb.

He stared at me and then thrust his finger at me, sneering. "You aren't even my son. Lewis is your father!"

Fireworks went off in my brain. Lewis, his younger brother, had died in Libya in a B-26 light bomber during World War II. Lewis is my middle name.

Was it possible?

Here was an explanation for his cruel treatment over the years, his bias toward Butch that I could never understand, and his anger at the coach who had suggested that Dad sponsor a team for a kid he didn't believe was his. It explained why he would be angry with Mom, and so many other things.

I didn't go into shock when he said that—I simply didn't believe him. But I think he believed it.

He may not have had any proof, but the thought must have tormented him. True or not, it didn't make any difference in my life. If it was true, no one else knew it. And regardless of whether he was right or wrong, his name was on my birth certificate.

In any case, it was not my fault.

When our dad finally ran out of steam, Butch and I left, shaking our heads, humiliated and ashamed of our dad. I wish I had had the courage to refuse to listen. He was destroying any respect I had left for him. I was tired of the way he treated people. He gave himself license to insult so many others, and not just his family, with his drunken rages.

I thought he had too many snakes in his head. He fought too many demons. Now, I knew some of the reasons why.

***

I heard nothing more from my father until Mom got really sick in the spring.

In April 1960 my mother underwent major surgery. She spent her thirty-sixth birthday in the hospital. By this time my dad was aware of her condition, and he visited her in the hospital and was civil about it as though he was really concerned. He was such a paradox.

One evening, Dad and all four of us siblings were at her bedside, which pleased her. She looked at us and then looked at her former husband and said, "We have such beautiful kids."

Dad replied, "Yes, we do," and she smiled.

That was the first positive exchange I had heard between the two of them in years. It made me feel better about them and myself.

Not long after that, I found myself at his home.

"Mike," he told me, "I just want you to know that your mother and I will be getting married when she gets well. I've spent a lot of time with her the last few days. We want to make things right."

I reasoned that if he really thought I was not his son, it would make things easier for both of them if I were not around. I told him that if they reunited, I would gladly go off to school somewhere.

Thinking I was being a smart aleck, he slapped me so hard that he burst my ear drum. With my ears ringing, I thought, "This guy must hate me."

Several years earlier, I had lost much of my hearing in my right ear to a mastoid infection, and with that slap I lost at least a third of the hearing in my left ear—and learned the definition of tinnitus the hard way.

About two weeks later, Dad called and instructed me to gather up my things and move in with him and my sisters. I was wary, but also relieved that I no longer had to live alone in the house on Windsor while my mom was hospitalized. The move meant transferring to Odessa High School, but I didn't mind because it reunited me with my family and brought me closer to Julie Richards.

We converted the den into my bedroom. I had my own door to the back yard and pool, and had a fold-out sofa-bed to sit on while doing my homework or smoking my pipe and reading Sherlock Holmes.

Those two months of school were pleasant enough; classes went well, and I planned to go to summer school to get caught up some even though I knew I would not graduate the next spring with my Permian High classmates. At least I would share the coming year with Odessa High people that I knew well in junior high school.

***

We went to the hospital daily to visit Mother. Home life with Dad seemed stable, and I dared to hope that the hardest times were behind us. Mother would get well and we would be a family again.

But my mother's surgeons did not solve all her problems. I stood by her bed one day as she moaned in pain while a fever raged. Doctors and nurses surrounded her with ice packs and cold, wet cloths. I could tell the nurses were worried that she was dying.

I found the hospital chapel, went in, closed the door, kneeled at the altar, and prayed that she would survive.

In a few minutes, peace came over me, and I suddenly felt like all was okay. I ran back up the stairway and saw the nurses leaving her room. One of them said, "The fever broke. She'll be okay for now."

I had never experienced anything like that before. I decided then and there that I would be more diligent about praying. That decision has stuck with me all my life, and over the years there have been other occasions when, against great odds, I got the same result. That will make a believer out of any doubting Thomas.

But the answer to that day's prayer was evidently for that crisis only. Some weeks later, Mom had yet another surgery. The pain and stress of repeated surgeries seemed to have turned her into an old woman overnight. When she was able to be moved, Dad brought her home and put her in his own bed. My sisters, Lea and Shirley, and I tended to her. Lea, our younger sister, was the saint. It was hard to get her away from her Mom.

In June, Mom suffered another crisis and begged my father for her pain pills.

He refused, saying, "Lillian, you're taking too many. You'll become addicted. You've got to cut back."

God, she looked gaunt and helpless and bony. Wild fear blazed in her eyes. She was fighting, but losing; her eyes told the truth. I wanted to tell her I loved her, but I was afraid she might think I was saying goodbye. I didn't want her to die; I wanted another miracle.

Her crying and pleading finally ran me out of the house and to the street, praying for a miracle. My sisters stayed inside, weeping beside her. Panicked, they begged Dad to give her the pain pills. He refused, but finally called an ambulance. Dad followed it to the hospital. He told us to stay home.

We went to bed and slept, but at dawn the next morning, June 10,

1960, we learned that our mother had died during the night. I was seventeen years old.

Years later, my sisters and I recalled the awful scene over the pain pills. The doctors had given them to her for pain relief, and Dad refused to let her have them. We all wondered if doing this meant Dad killed our mother that night. No one should have to go out of this world like she did, screaming in agony.

I would rather she had died with an overdose than with no damned pills at all. She was terminally ill; Dad was worried about a dying woman becoming addicted? I didn't understand. Neither did my two sisters. We were crushed.

My mom's death was like a cannon ball shot through my chest, leaving a gaping hole of emptiness. She was my protector, but now she was gone, forever. I had to accept the fact that from then on I would have to navigate some tricky waters with my volatile, alcoholic father without her.

My mother's well-attended funeral was held in a large Methodist church where many people knew her. When her favorite hymn, Rock of Ages, was played, all of us kids wept openly. After the service, we all drove to the cemetery, escorted by two young policemen we knew who had volunteered to lead the procession.

Then it was over.

Except it wasn't. The hole in the chest never quite heals, even over a long life. Shrouded in grief and a multitude of other emotions, victimhood crept into my being and I was never given a clue on how to deal with it. It was too embedded in grief to recognize it.

And more hell was coming.

***

The June of mother's death, I actually passed a biology course in summer school. I have no idea how I stayed focused enough to do that, but I pressed on hoping life would look up for everyone in our family.

I don't think my dad showed any grief over my mother's death. He had had a lady in his life named Petey before he and Mother agreed to remarry. Soon after Mom died, Petey became a frequent visitor in our home; I wondered if Dad wanted us to accept her. She was an intelligent bookkeeper and lived alone not far from us.

There were times when Dad would disappear during the afternoon, and I often saw his car in her driveway. I was not surprised, nor was I disappointed. That was their business, and they had known each other throughout my parents' divorce. Deep down, I thought Dad might be easier to live with if he had someone like her in his life. I liked her and her influence on my dad.

Julie Richards had a sorority sister who lived next door to my dad's house, and Julie visited her occasionally. One day I watched from behind a curtain as Julie parked her car, gathered some notebooks, and then ever so slightly cast a side glance at our house.

My heart quickened and seemed to skip a beat. I had seen her through my tears at Mom's funeral. Maybe she still cared.

I thought about asking Dad for some money and the use of one of the cars so I could ask her out. Even though I still had my blue

Chevy, my dad had made it clear that I had to have permission for everything.

I tip-toed on eggshells in fear of upsetting him. I worried that money was scarce.

As June turned into July and August, Dad's business phone rang less and less often. I hoped he had some plan, but said nothing. I had no idea how much money he had in reserve, if any.

Right before school started he called me aside and said, "Mike, money's tight. We'll going to have to sell your car. You kids need new clothes for school."

Dad sold the car for five hundred dollars and gave my sisters two hundred dollars each, and I got one hundred.

I assumed he would give me the company car since no one was using it, but it didn't happen. To get to school, we drove Mother's car, a white 1957 Chrysler four-door hardtop. With that car, I thought I might have a shot at a social life and reconciliation with Julie. Hope springs eternal in the heart of youth.

Nothing disastrous happened during the first month of September, though it seemed that the less his phone rang, the more alcohol Dad consumed. When he drank, we all went to our rooms and were quiet, not wanting to challenge him in any way.

One night he got so soused that after he took a shower he fell down face first on his bed and passed out, stark naked. I pulled the covers over him and closed his bedroom door, disgusted but relieved that we would not have to avoid him all evening.

One night Dad, sober for a change, suggested that he and I get a milkshake. I drove the company car, a brown and white '57 Chevy. He directed me to a very old drive-in, one of the first in Odessa. It was built of dark sandstone and reminded me of a castle. I think Dad and his generation might have hung out there when he was my age. The carhop took our orders: a strawberry milkshake for me, chocolate for him. We had never done anything like this before that I could remember. It excited me to sit this way with my dad, just the two of us, having a congenial conversation.

Talk turned to his philosophy of the role of the father. He explained that he saw himself as a hub, like that of a wagon wheel, and he drew this on a napkin. He saw the kids as the spokes of the wheel, and as the hub he was the center of experience and authority. In order for the kids to avoid life's shocks, mistakes, and tragedies, they should consult their dad for advice on every issue. In other words, he wanted us to be totally dependent on him, rather than growing in experience and independence.

"Dad," I countered, trying not to appear argumentative, "if you make all the decisions, how can I ever learn how to make my own? Your way just creates doubts. And what would happen if you were suddenly killed in a car wreck?"

I went on. "I have to learn to trust my own judgment sometime, Dad."

He didn't respond. He just got a frustrated look on his face. I feared he just thought me stupid, and the atmosphere turned sullen.

First and foremost, I believed his family model exemplified a need for absolute control over the lives of everyone around him. Period.

But his experiences could not be transferred into my brain, and I thought it strange that he could not see that. Furthermore, I saw that some of my friends were given more independence, and things were working out just fine for them and their parents. Why could I see that and he could not?

My seventeen-year-old brain concluded that the ultimate maturity was to believe in my own sound judgment and not have to rely on a parent. Did he think he would live forever? Didn't Mother's death affect his view of his own mortality? Who guided him up to now, and how did he get so wise? Here I was, less than one year away from being a legal adult, and my dad was trying to convince me that the way to adulthood was to be a puppet on his string.

Something was not connecting here. He appeared to be headed for financial disaster and he was doing nothing about it. He didn't seem to have a clue as to how to make a living in a souring economy.

The truth is that he had had no guidance; whatever he learned, he learned on his own. I saw the whole conversation as an explanation for his need for control.

For instance, he would secretly follow the girls to and from the movies to make sure they came home exactly the way he directed them to, and not one minute later than when he told them to be home. I wish now that I had had the courage to point out to him that he might be the only parent in Odessa who thought that was necessary.

I think I remember this incident so vividly for two reasons. The first is how fast my hope was dashed that he and I could have a mature dialogue where some agreement could be reached. The second was the realization that he and I were hopelessly at philosophical odds. I think he saw me that night as hopelessly stubborn, and probably dim-witted. Although there were no raised voices, the conversation ended with mutual frustration that did not bode well for the future.

***

That summer we brought my only living grandmother, Mom's mother, into Dad's home where we kids nursed her back from some kind of physical crisis. I never knew exactly what it was that nearly killed her, but in retrospect I have wondered if she hadn't simply nearly stressed herself to death with the loss of her only child.

Looking back, I have suspected her of overdosing on alcohol to assuage her grief, though I had never known her or her husband, our Grandfather Stewart, to drink, and I had been around them more than any other member of our family.

In a matter of days, she made a miraculous recovery under our care, and soon she went back to her home in Monahans, thirty-seven miles away, where she owned and ran a liquor store.

Meanwhile, I was just a powerless teenager wondering if his dad could take care of his children financially.

The answer came on an autumn-edged night during the first week of October 1960. Dad was hitting the Scotch fairly heavily again. He and Lea were on the other side of the house, arguing. Shirley came home five minutes late and was also chastised.

This was nothing unusual, but this time I could hear Shirley protest. Their voices grew louder. Then I heard yelling and screaming and a loud thump against a wall.

Oh no!

I ran to Shirley's bedroom. Dad had pinned Shirley against the wall, his hands around her neck and her toes barely touching the floor. I pulled him off and he turned on me like a rabid dog.

I was seventeen and no weakling. I was behind him, and he flailed at me over his left shoulder, trying to hit me with his fist. We fell on the bed, and his hand came up to my face.

I bit his hand, hard. I tasted blood and knew he was in pain. I yelled for the girls to call the police.

Even as we struggled, I recognized that I had crossed a line. Things had never escalated to this point before, and I had never dared to engage my own father in a physical altercation.

There would be hell to pay.

He was not the type to forgive, and I had done the unforgiveable. More violence was likely in the future. I knew I would be his next target.

We kids would have to leave.

Lordy, this was insane. I hadn't tried to win a battle here; I was just determined not to watch or take a beating! He was wrong to physically abuse the girls, and though I was scared and angry, he had left me no choice but to stop him.

Thankfully, a police officer arrived quickly, and we disengaged.

The alcohol Dad had consumed earlier gave him the courage to get verbally abusive with the policeman, who took him to jail for the night. Shirley, Lea, and I quickly agreed that we would go to our grandmother's house in Monahans, thirty-seven miles to the west.

We put our belongings in Mother's 1957 Chrysler, and we went to the only destination we thought logical. We were three wide-eyed teenagers on that trip, saying little, knowing that our lives had just changed forever.

It was close to midnight when, shaken and bewildered, we banged on our grandmother's door. Taking in the scene through sleepy eyes, she asked, "What happened? What did he do?"

I let the girls talk, and she stood there, absorbing their stories.

When they finished, she scowled and said, "I wondered if it would finally come to this."

She shook her head. "That son of a bitch."

I said nothing, but her words proved to me that I was not alone in what I saw in our father. She had known all along that he had snakes in his head. I unloaded our clothes from the car and carried them into our new bedrooms.

It had been another hellacious day. Would this ever end?

The next morning, we three rattled teenagers marched into a new life by enrolling ourselves at Monahans High School. We plunged into a world of new people and bewildering challenges that we faced by just hanging on one day at a time.

We wondered just what the hell awaited us next.

CHAPTER 8

HITTING BOTTOM

We quickly saw that our grandmother was a drinker. I had never in my life seen her or her late husband take a sip of anything alcoholic. Now she drank vodka all day.

By the time we got home from school she was blasted. She could be vulgar when she was drunk, and gradually, over weeks that turned into months, her drunkenness became a permanent state.

I often wondered if the recent death of her daughter caused her to go in that direction. Shirley and I would find her stash after she passed out in her bed, and we would empty the bottle down the sink and then refill it with water. That was a mean thing to do, but hell, how else could we send her the message?

This prankster stuff enraged her, and we would argue with her over her drinking. She just got meaner and uglier. She became someone I didn't know. I saw insanity everywhere I looked in the adult world around us.

To top things off, big brother Butch showed up a few days after we had moved in with Grandma. Here we were, Shirley, Lea, and I, stuck in Monahans, living with a self-destructing, alcoholic grandmother after fleeing from a self-destructing, violent father in Odessa. Mom's 1957 Chrysler was the only possession we had that represented a path out of the mess we were in. Selfish and entitled, Butch thought it should be his.

I had borrowed my grandmother's car to go to the library. As I returned to the house I saw Butch's wife pulling away in their car and wondered what the hell was going on.

Mom's car was in the carport. As I pulled up, Butch, with a sheepish look, was opening the driver's door. Shirley and Lea stood in the carport, wide-eyed.

Shirley blurted out, "Mike, Butch is taking Mom's car."

I was aghast. I know Butch knew it from the bewildered look on my face. I realized that our father had told him where we were, and why.

"You guys will be all right," he said as he started the car. "I've got to go." He backed out without looking at us.

We were now stranded with no way to leave without the help of someone else, and I had no idea who that might be.

Butch sold the car and kept all the money.

***

Toward the end of the fall semester at Monahans, I showed my sisters the requirements for graduation compared to those for Odessa High. Monahans required more credits. I told them I would be better off if I went back to Odessa. They were okay with that.

I told Alford Smallwood and Cameron Ray my thoughts one weekend during the Christmas holidays when I got a ride into Odessa. Cameron immediately called his parents, who said I would be welcome in their home. I hitched a ride back to Monahans, told my sisters, and started packing.

I don't remember how my grandmother felt about it. I rather think she was fed up with teenagers interfering with her drinking.

Soon after that, my sisters had a huge blow-up with our alcoholic grandmother. Dad moved them into an apartment in Monahans and hired a nanny to stay with them, but it didn't take long for the money to run out. Two sympathetic families in Monahans took the girls in until school was out for the summer. It was more head-shaking shame for us.

My new roommate, Cameron Ray, was a tall, thin guy with coal black hair and brown eyes. He knew he was intelligent.

The rental home we lived in housed nine people: Cameron's parents, Cameron and his three younger brothers and two younger sisters, and me.

Cameron and I shared a small bedroom, and we both worked part-time at the service station his dad managed. We often closed up at nine o'clock before going home to do our homework. His parents bought a used 1957 Chevrolet four-door sedan for us to commute to school.

Familiar faces from junior high greeted me when I started the 1961 spring semester at Permian High. My old junior high classmates were now seniors, though I was classified as a junior since I had lost a year after dropping out during my sophomore year. It was tempting to join the old circle, but I purposely kept to myself, because all I had time for was homework and my afternoon job at the station.

Cameron did the same, but his life was taking a different direction. He lost interest in school when he fell in love. Cameron and his girlfriend, Aline, wanted to get married, but they had no money. I told Cameron about my uncle, an oil driller in South Texas, who might pay him a third more an hour than the minimum wage we got at the service station.

Cameron quit school, took the job, and left Odessa. He left his car for me to use. It felt strange to stay with his parents without him, but I was made to feel welcome, especially by his tender-hearted mother, Willie Beth.

***

Midway through the semester, achievement tests were administered over a two-day period. For the first time ever in high school I cared about what scores I made, and I gave it my best, thinking nothing about it.

A few weeks later I was called out of class to the principal's office. I headed that way wondering what kind of trouble I was in. I was told to take a seat and wait.

Finally, the door opened. Tall and bald, the principal studied me for a moment and then silently hooked his finger at the room behind him. Looking serious, he closed the door behind me.

He sat at his desk and opened a file, stared at it, and then stared at another file next to it. He leaned back in his chair and looked me in the eye.

"How did you cheat on your achievement tests?" he said.

Cheat? I was dumbfounded. "Sir, I have no idea how a student could even cheat on such a test!"

"Me, neither," he said. He tapped the file. "If you were copying someone else's answers you would have been caught. We've seen it all."

"I didn't cheat, sir," I insisted.

He looked at me long and steady and finally spoke, "I believe you."

He rubbed his chin. "You are sitting here, Mike, because neither I nor your teachers knew you were this kind of student."

"Honestly, sir, I never cared to try on these tests before." I didn't tell him why. Nor did I explain I had been severely distracted for a long time by family dysfunction. I had to keep that a secret.

"I believe you on that score, too." He closed the file folders and smiled. "You are excused. Have a good day."

I was surprised when I was shown the scores. I was previously a piss-poor high school student due to the hell in my life. Except for math, these new scores were in the lower ninety percentiles. I pondered where I would be if I had chosen to use academics rather than cars as my escape from dysfunction.

What if, when I was in the ninth grade and going steady with Julie, I had told her up front, from the very beginning of the tough times, that I wanted to survive by being the best student I could be? She probably would have tutored me, and I would have kept her as a girlfriend and made her proud.

But being a great student would not have generated a roof over my head or meals on my plate. So I drew no conclusions from my speculations. Maybe I hadn't really failed. Maybe it was a bad economy and my parents who had failed, not me.

That spring, while I lived with the Ray family, my grandmother died. Butch, Shirley, Lea, and I were together at the graveside service in Monahans.

Cameron's mother approached us as we watched our grandmother's casket being lowered into the ground. As shovelfuls of earth covered it, Willie Beth Ray, that saintly woman, said to us, "You kids have all been through hell, and none of it has been your fault."

She was the only adult I ever heard say that out loud.

***

When the semester was over, Cameron returned to Odessa and he and Aline got married. He reclaimed his car, which left me once more without transportation. I thought it wasn't fair for me to continue to live with his parents when Cameron no longer lived there, but I was still working part-time for minimum wage and was nearly broke.

Two weeks went by as I wondered what to do. When our grandmother died, she left each of us kids four thousand dollars, but it was not to be distributed to us until we turned twenty-one. Those three years might as well have been a lifetime—I hadn't finished high school, had no transportation, and was relying on the kindness of friends for a place to live.

I was working at the service station one day when my brother Butch came by. He and his wife were once again on the outs, and I suggested we go to South Texas and work for our uncle. He agreed.

In those few seconds my life took a different heading. We quickly packed and headed to Three Rivers, Texas. Butch had a fairly new 1960 Chevrolet convertible and he drove it like a demon, fleeing from his wife and kids and the turmoil at home.

Our uncle quickly put us to work on the floor of his oil rig. Butch and I found a room with two beds in the home of an elderly, spinster piano teacher. I liked her, and over the summer as I spent time with her, we got to know each other. In August, when it was time to go back to Odessa so I could try to find a way to finish high school, she offered me the room free of charge. I was touched, and I hugged her, but I thought my chances of finishing school were better on familiar ground, so Butch and I returned to Odessa.

I was convinced that I never wanted to try to make a living in an oil patch, and I definitely wanted to go to college, but I had no idea how I could do it.

***

In Odessa, Butch reconciled with his wife. They did not ask me to live with them, which was fine with me because I had no good feelings for his spouse, and the feeling was mutual.

But Butch came up with a solution to my predicament. He had learned about a vacant trailer house that belonged to the parents of one of his friends.

He took me there and left me, alone and on my own. I didn't have two cents in my pocket.

The trailer represented the bottom of the barrel for me. It sat in a trailer park at the far edge of town, adjacent to the Odessa Country Club, where I had spent so many good times dating those wonderful young ladies during junior high.

To be invited there with my friends, and to go to their parties and be a part of their lives, had been so special, and my life had been so different then. Now, I could look out the rear window of that trailer house and see that country club with its lush golf course and manicured grounds. It might as well have been a million miles away and a hundred years ago when those things happened.

How far away I was from where I once was, and from where I someday might choose to be! I sat alone in the back bedroom of that trailer working on another severe case of depression.

I was broke from staying in motels and eating all my meals out. In the front of the unkempt trailer was a driveway, but I had no car to put in it. I had no way to get to school or work. I had no home, no mother, and no dad who cared where I was. I had no grandparents.

I didn't seem to have any close relationships. I had no idea where my poor, shell-shocked sisters were. I hoped they were faring better than I was. The new school year was starting in a few days and none of my high school friends even knew where I was. I wanted to finish high school, but I couldn't see how I could do it.

There was only one thing left to do, and that was to go to the Air Force recruiter's office, which I did by bumming a ride with a stranger who lived in the trailer next door.

He started his car, backed out and stayed on the service road into town. "Where are we going?"

"I need to go to the Air Force Recruiter's office near, Second Street and Grant."

"I know where it is. You're not joining up, are you?"

"I have to." I took a deep breath. "I don't have a choice."

He raised his eyebrows. "Are you in trouble?"

I chuckled. "No. I'm not in any kind of legal trouble. It's a long story. A lot of people, grownups in my life, have died. I'm just out of luck, that's all. I just need to go in a different direction."

He looked at me and said nothing. He pulled up to the recruiter's office and parked. "I'll wait on you," he offered. "I have the time. I just drove in to get a six pack."

I checked in, filled out a form, took a number and sat down and waited among several other young men. Finally, my name was called, and I was directed into a small office where a middle-aged man in uniform sat at his desk.

He directed me to a chair and asked about my background. I told him what I had told my driver.

The recruiter considered what I had said and replied, "Mike, you need to finish high school. This branch of the service would have to make an exception for you unless you scored very high on our entry tests."

I countered, "I want to take the tests, sir. I just don't have any alternatives. I love airplanes. I don't want the other branches of service."

He nodded and said, "You'll have to come back Monday morning to take the tests. It's too late in the day now, and I want you to think about this, too."

On the way home, my trailer park neighbor stopped at a convenience store and got his beer, and then he took us both back to the trailer camp, where he offered me a bottle. I thanked him, but I didn't want any of his beer on an empty stomach, and I sure didn't want him feeling sorry for me.

Depressed, I slept a lot the next day, a Saturday. Late in the day I was desperately hungry, so I scavenged the trailer and found a can of broth. It wasn't mine, but I had to have something, so I cleaned up a pan and heated it up. It was better than nothing. I went back to bed and tossed and turned through a long night.

Sunday morning finally crawled into the stinky trailer. I just needed for Monday to come so I could disappear out of town on an Air Force bus without saying goodbye to anyone. I lay on the bed. There was nothing better to do, and besides, moving around just made me more aware of how empty my stomach was.

I had more problems than a stump-tail bull in a swarm of flies. Thanks, Dad.

Towards noon I heard a car pull into the driveway. A car door slammed and footsteps crunched on the gravel, and before I could get to it, the front door opened. Alford Smallwood, the guy I considered my best friend, stomped into the trailer and looked around. He wrinkled his nose at the dirty, mildewed clothes and filthy kitchen and bathroom.

"Get your stuff together," he said. "You're going home with me. We're going to finish high school."

As we drove, I turned my head away from Alford so he couldn't see the lump in my throat and tears of relief that formed. We passed the cemetery where my mother was buried and I studied the passing landscape.

I was relieved beyond words, but wondered if this would end up being yet another disappointment.

Alford said nothing as he drove. He seemed angry. I guessed he was mad about the mess I was in. When we got to his house, we got out of the car, walked straight through the front door, and he announced to his surprised parents that I was going to stay with him and that we would sleep in the well house.

They both jumped up to welcome me, and the four of us went to work rearranging things so I would have a place to live.

In the blink of an eye, my life had changed drastically yet again.

CHAPTER 9

A SHOT AT A NEW LIFE

The Smallwood family home was only about seven hundred square feet. In the back yard was the well house, an uninsulated wooden structure built around the galvanized steel tank that sat on top of their water well. Besides keeping the water tank from freezing in cold weather, it served as a storage shed for the family's odds and ends.

We started pulling things out, and Alford's mom and dad worked right beside us. After sweeping the cement floor as clean as it could be swept, Alford put together a steel bed frame and stacked an old mattress from the collection on it. His mom brought sheets and blankets from the house, and we made up the bed. Alford strung a clothes line for me to hang my clothes on, and that was it. We had our penthouse!

I wasn't going to join the Air Force after all. I had a new home, and would start school the next day.

Alford's mother was known as Muzzie to those close to her. She produced many wonderful meals in her small kitchen, and the meal she served that night marked the first sit-down, normal supper I had eaten in weeks. I thought I had never tasted something so good.

Muzzie was a wonderful cook, and Alford let her know it. After the last bite was swallowed, he tipped back in his chair and smiled at his mother through the smoke from his after-meal cigarette and complained, as he always did, that he had eaten too much good food. She blushed at the attention, but I think she loved it.

It was Sunday night, the last day of summer vacation before the semester began. Alford looked at me and said. "Let's go to Tommy's."

We sprang up from the kitchen table, took our dishes to the sink, and I think there was a wink from Alford to his quiet, gray-haired, saintly

little mother that told her he would do the dishes the following night. In fact, he knew that I would be initiated into taking turns with him and his younger brother, Millard,

Mike

Alford

for dish duty the coming year. But I realized that we also needed to get out of the house so his parents could talk about what it meant for their household to suddenly take on another teenager.

As we drove the few blocks to Tommy's Drive-In, I considered how fortunate I was not to be on a bus to San Antonio to join a branch of the military service in order to have a place to eat and sleep. I knew that tomorrow I would enroll in Odessa High School and finish the last few courses I needed.

A new chapter was starting. I had to manage the best I could.

***

The fight I got into that night at Tommy's was not the best introduction to that new chapter of my life, but the Smallwoods seemed to understand that the stranger's challenge had unleashed in me a well of anger and grief and frustration that I had tried to keep under wraps for so long. They never mentioned it, and I think they knew it wouldn't happen again.

At school, Alford and I were taken into a good crowd, and schoolwork became important to me. We both wanted out of high school with a diploma in our hands. We had already had all the non-academic fun we could stand in our earlier years, and all that fun had put us into the humbling position that we now found ourselves.

In some ways Alford and I became like two grumpy old men around any wise guys who would cut up in class and hinder our path to graduation. It was funny, especially since there were some teachers and counselors who wondered why we even bothered to show up, considering our performance when we were sophomores.

But we hung in there and graduated, albeit a year late, with the Odessa High School Class of 1962.

* * *

The Smallwood family loved each other, and they loved their friends. No one was chronically stressed or mad. Everyone who knew them admired them. If there was a defining characteristic of Alford Smallwood, it was the fact that if you were his friend, you knew he loved you.

The ladies loved him, too.

My life in the Smallwood home was a profound contrast to my past. They accepted me as a family member, and I relished the peaceful atmosphere. There was none of the fighting and tension and uncertainty I had lived with the last three years.

At last, I had found a normal life.

Muzzie had a garden in the back yard that Alford, Millard, and I had tilled and kept weed-free under the sharp eyes of Archie, Alford's father. Black-eyed peas that we had shelled were often included in the supper menu, which nearly always consisted of fried potatoes, pinto beans, cornbread, cream gravy, and some kind of meat.

Of course, any beans or peas on the table would have been cooked in a pot with ample bacon, and probably butter, and they were no doubt artistically flavored with salt and black pepper. Muzzie never had to worry about leftovers.

With three teenage boys at the table every night, suppers were somewhat competitive, though in a subtle way. Millard, Alford, and I quietly chomped down our food with an eye on each other to see who would be first to get a second helping of fried potatoes.

Don't get me wrong; I am not implying that there was not enough to eat in that small house. I am sure it was just assumed by both parents that too much would have never been enough, because we no doubt looked like three desperate wolves eating like we might never have the chance again. It was often a race among the three boys to see who could out-hog the others on those potatoes, yet we maintained a very controlled effort not to appear too anxious or boorish or totally uncouth.

But the competition was there, and all three of us would quietly, and with focused attention, put away what we had on our plates after taking a fair share on the first go-around. We boys were physically very active, both during school hours with P.E. class, and afterwards, playing some type of sandlot sport, and by the time supper came around, we were famished. I remember Archie and Muzzie watching in silence, both no doubt amazed at how much food could go down the throats of three young guys.

***

Most evenings, after the meal Muzzie would set out a pie that she had made that day, usually apple or cherry. I seldom ate pie, thinking that it was so obviously relished by Archie and his two sons that I did not want to add to the competition for it. Somehow, I thought they might believe I didn't like desserts. Little did they know how wrong they were.

One evening after I had lived with them for about six months, Archie, Muzzie, Alford, and Millard went to visit a sick family member in the hospital. The three of us boys always took turns doing dishes, and I told them I would finish up.

I guess being alone in their house for the first time gave me a somewhat new feeling, one of solitude, or maybe it was a moment of privacy I hadn't experienced while living with them. I can't explain it, but the word liberty comes to mind—as if I was no longer a guest of sorts, but more like a member of the family.

I cleared the dinner table and started putting the dishes beside the sink as I filled it with hot soapy water. The TV was on in the small living room, but I paid no attention to it. I am sure I was daydreaming and enjoying being alone in the house when my eyes drifted over to the right of the sink, past the dish rack, to that place near the black, rotary dial telephone, right below the cupboard, where an untouched cherry pie sat.

Surely, I thought, after all these months of turning down a piece of cherry pie, no one would notice if I took a small piece. After all, it was not even my turn to do the dishes. I was doing either Alford or Millard a big favor by stepping up and doing the dishes for him.

So, strengthened with logic and emboldened with righteousness, I took a dinner knife and cut a small slice of pie and put it on a saucer, and as I leaned back up against the kitchen counter, fork in hand and totally alone, I luxuriously ate some of the best pie anyone ever ate, one delicious bite after another.

Muzzie was a great cook.

I then returned to the now dragged-out task of finishing the dinner dishes. I was in no hurry because the time was mine, and doing dishes is not something easy to do with gusto anyway. And now the pie sat there in its usual place with just one small piece missing.

"Just one piece," I thought.

That might look odd to Muzzie when they returned, and she would wonder which one among her family members had eaten it. Again I reasoned, quite logically, that it would make more sense if two pieces were missing, because then she would think that both Alford and Millard had gotten their dessert before going to the hospital.

It only made sense to eat another piece. So, now things would be okay, and no one would sense anything out of the ordinary. I cut just a little bigger piece this time, and I loved it all over again.

This dishwashing thing was going slowly, and my mind was wandering, and my enjoyment of the liberty and privacy was just so satisfying that I didn't want it to end too prematurely. And I began to think again.

There would be nothing wrong with Muzzie concluding that both of her boys had eaten a piece of pie before going to the hospital, and for Mike to have eaten a piece while they were all gone; so I took another piece, slightly bigger yet, since I had so seldom eaten any pie in all those months before.

After that piece was gone, and my taste buds were humming, I assumed that Alford and Millard would have wanted the same size piece of pie that I had just eaten, or else they would have felt cheated, so I evened out their shares by taking yet another little slice.

I was getting into trouble now and I knew it. But what was a guy to do?

Then an absolutely brilliant thought hit me.

It was the only way out. I would eat the final two slices of that cherry pie, clean up the pie plate, wash it, dry it, and put it back in the cupboard. Muzzie would forget that she had made a pie that day!

I rationalized that she had a lot on her mind with sick relatives. My energy level was rising, and I stepped up the pace as I finished the dishes and nipped away at the pie until the crumbs and crust and everything were gone—out of mind and out of sight, in my belly.

I furiously cleaned the kitchen up a little more than usual to make it look good to Muzzie, thinking that she would spend her time remembering how hard I had tried to please her rather than letting her mind dwell on the question of whether or not she might have made a pie that day.

Determined logic in the face of temptation is an amazing thing.

Still alone, but not quite so euphoric and starting to wonder when the family might return, my mood changed, and reality started to creep like a devilish shadow into my mind. I began questioning whether or not I had made an irreparably bad mistake.

Well, there was only one thing to do, and that was to bathe and go to bed early and be sound asleep when the Smallwoods got back home. So that's what I did.

Soon, while I was trying to force myself to sleep, I heard their car pull into the driveway. I remember hearing their voices in the house and lights coming on in the kitchen as I pretended to fall deeper into slumber.

After a while, I heard the screen door slam, and I assumed it was Alford coming to bed in the well house. He came in and undressed while I still pretended to be deeply asleep, but I didn't fool him.

As he pulled up the covers, he said, "Well, I hope you enjoyed the pie." In a few minutes he was sound asleep, obviously with a clear conscience. I lay awake with my eyes closed and worried about the repercussions.

The next morning, when I finally went into the kitchen in the main house, Alford and Millard kidded me good-naturedly. Muzzie just laughed with them and shook her head. I was incredibly relieved that they saw humor in it all, though I was thoroughly embarrassed.

Later, during that final semester of high school, I had to write a two-page paper in my English class, and chose the story of Muzzie's cherry pie and my pitiful logic. The teacher had always seemed to like only football players and cheerleaders, and I was neither, but when she handed our papers back, mine had the highest grade I had yet earned in her class.

I gave Muzzie the paper as sort of a confession. Bless her heart; she was pleased. I think it tickled and flattered her that I thought her cooking was that good.

***

I was Alford's shadow. Without him I had no car. I found a part-time job working some evenings and on weekends at a service station, but without a car of my own I was dependent on Alford.

I was ecstatic when I ferreted out a beat-up '57 Ford pickup that Dad had abandoned at the old Notrees home site. By this time, Dad had declared bankruptcy, but the truck had not been considered an asset. Its frame was bent, but I got it running, put used tires on it and serviced it, and put new tags on it, all paid for with the part-time wages I had saved.

It was only halfway presentable, but at last I had wheels!

What a dreamer I was. I have no idea how Dad found out that I had fixed up the truck, but a few days later he came and got it for himself, telling me emphatically, "It is my pickup, you know!"

He didn't even offer to reimburse the money I had sunk into it, though I suspected he had no money with which to do so.

Still, I may have dodged another bullet with that old battered pickup; it wasn't long until he wrecked it again. He rolled it over and sustained injuries that nagged him the rest of his life.

By this time, he had become an itinerant alcoholic. He had no home that I knew of. Every good value my dad had ever held was no longer important to him. When he gave up, he gave up everything, including his self-respect and any concern for his struggling kids. I guess he was struggling, too.

It was a delicious feeling of freedom knowing he could not control me anymore. Though he was still an influence in my life, I was now a legal adult, calling my own shots, and in the care of normal people until I could get into college.

My life was mine, not his.

As tough as times were, I never thought about stealing or cheating or doing anything bad. It never occurred to me; I reasoned that if I did, and got caught, no one would be willing to take a worthless lout into their home.

Why help someone who did not do the right thing? I felt my only value to anyone was in my moral make-up. I figured that if I was a good person, I would always have a chance. If I needed help, someone would help me, as long as I was a *good person.*

That thought became a survival tool for life. It kept me on track and made me more of an adult than a kid, but there was still plenty of kid left in me who wanted something of the normal social life I had missed during the last three years.

One spring Saturday afternoon I was reading a book in the well house when Muzzie called me to the phone in the main house. I couldn't imagine who it might be; hardly anyone ever called for me.

I picked up the receiver and was surprised to hear Cameron Ray's mother, Willie Beth. Her soft, West Texas accent came over the line: "Mike, you are about to graduate, and you need a car.

"I want to offer you a loan of $700," she said. "You can pay me back when you get to be twenty-one and get the money your grandmother left you. Come over to the house and sign a note, and I'll give you a check. Start looking for a car."

Stunned, I accepted her offer and thanked her, then stepped into the back yard and choked back tears of relief and gratitude.

Willie Beth was a mother of five who watched her pennies and didn't have a lot of extras, and yet she was offering this to me, who was not even her own child. The words *she cares!* exploded in my head.

It was one of the most profound emotional experiences I have ever had. Today, I still feel the strength of emotion when I recall that moment. I put the story in writing, and it was read as part of the eulogy at her funeral when she died in her nineties.

Things were going well at last, thanks to people who cared.

CHAPTER 10

STEPS FORWARD, STEPS BACKWARD

During the last weeks of the spring semester, when graduation was the focus, I remember thinking that maybe, just maybe, Dad would be proud of the first of his kids to complete high school.

My classmates were getting nice graduation presents: new cars, trips, parties in their homes, and the like. I knew that real life was just beginning for me. I could "catch up" with my classmates, and somewhere, deep down, I thought Dad was going to give me a surprise gift for graduation. Maybe he would want me to have a new car for college, or maybe a better car. Hope springs eternal in the heart of youth.

He found me right before all the graduates were to line up and enter the field house for the ceremony. Out of the corner of my eye, I spied a familiar figure ambling toward me. My heart thumped. Maybe the surprise was at hand after all. My Dad—he cared!

Sure enough, he had a surprise for me. With an uncomfortable look on his face he asked to "borrow" twenty dollars of the graduation money he figured I had in my pocket.

Stunned, I gave it to him.

A few minutes later, I followed my classmates into the field house where I would at last graduate from high school and be eligible to go on to college. I was thrilled to be there, but it was a bittersweet occasion knowing I was twenty dollars poorer so my old man could get drunk again.

It was the last time I ever had a feeling of any expectation from him. In a way I had become the caretaker, and he was just a taker.

Nevertheless, the graduation experience was pure euphoria. I had spent all four of my high school years without competent adult supervision from any of my family and had still managed to graduate in spite of all the meltdowns and my own lack of confidence and self-discipline.

How many people can say that? I had a car, a part-time job, a high school diploma, and an inheritance from my grandmother that might make college possible.

***

I had a plan.

In my new (used) car I drove to nearby Monahans and went to the bank that administered the funds our grandmother had left to us kids. I got an audience with the president and explained that I wanted to go to college in the fall.

He agreed to pay for books and tuition from my share of the inheritance. I was going to go to college! I was thrilled that he understood my predicament.

My old flame, Julie Richards, had just finished her freshman year at TCU in Fort Worth. It was important to me to let her know that at last, I was proud of myself. I wanted her to know that I had stuck in there and done the right thing and was planning to go to college that fall.

I was invited to a couple of parties celebrating classmates' graduations and with fingers crossed, I gambled and called her up. When she consented to go to a party with me, I was higher than Ben Franklin's kite. We spent the evening together at the Odessa Country Club, chatting with friends by the pool in a perfect desert night.

I was euphoric.

It was just before midnight when I parked my car in front of Julie's house for the first time in four long years. I turned off the engine and leaned up against the door and just looked at her. She was sitting close to me. She leaned into me a bit and raised her face to me, and I kissed her. She was in my arms again.

I felt like I was washing away all the grimness of the previous four years without her in my life. I held her, letting those feelings flood over me. It was heaven for a few moments, and in fact, after the evening was over and I went home to my well-house bedroom apartment, I slept like I had not slept since the first night I told her I loved her. Still, I sensed an uneasiness from her, but I hoped to change that if she would let me.

We had more dates that summer, which made the time almost as much fun as when we dated while in junior high. For me, our time together was almost surreal. I was so thankful to be with her once more. We laughed together about the song "The Second Time Around."

I even surprised her with a ring, a very small diamond in a Tiffany setting that she talked about seeing in the window of a pawnshop downtown. She liked it, and thanked me, but didn't indicate that she considered it anything more than a gift.

We often hung out at one of the quiet drive-ins in town to sip a Coke and talk. I'd leave the radio in my '55 Chevy turned down low, maybe to fill awkward moments of silence. More than once my stomach knotted when Floyd Cramer's instrumental, "The Last Date," came over the airwaves, because deep down I knew that every date I had with Julie could well be the last.

Just the title of that mournful piece pierced me, and I hardly needed to hear any words, but when the song was sung the words went right through me.

Julie had another guy in her life. I knew she was emotionally conflicted, but hope springs eternal in the heart of a desperate lover like me.

The state of denial was better than facing the truth, so I plodded onward through the summer and part of the fall, hoping for a miracle.

***

That fall, I teamed up with an old classmate and decided to follow him to Tarleton State University, in Stephenville, just sixty miles from Fort Worth and Julie at TCU.

While I was at Tarleton, in one of her letters to me, Julie reiterated that she did not really know me. I had never told her about my hard times. I wrote back and tried to describe some of the ghosts from my past.

In her next letter, she said something to the effect that what I told her made her want to run and scream. When I read that, I thought that maybe I had been right about not dragging her through my mess. Maybe I had done the right thing by breaking up with her and sparing her any involvement with me during those difficult years.

I will never know.

One evening in early December, I drove to Fort Worth to see Julie. Somehow I knew she would be studying at the TCU library, and I found her there. She was surprised, but she smiled and immediately closed her books, and together we walked out to my car in the dark parking lot.

We chatted but something was different. The spark in her was not as bright, and she seemed more distant.

I sensed that she had made a decision.

There were no jobs for me in Stephenville, and I had saved enough money for only one semester unless I also had a job. So after one semester at Tarleton State, almost out of the money I'd saved over the summer, I had to return to Odessa.

Back in Odessa during the Christmas holiday, I asked Julie again for a date. When she got into my car, for the first time ever she did not move to the middle of the seat next to me. The body language was unmistakable.

I don't remember where we went or what we did or talked about, but I vividly recall walking her to her front door at the end of the evening. I wanted to tell her that I had never, ever, stopped loving her like she thought I had years earlier when I broke up with her. I wanted to tell her that whatever good I was or ever did was mostly because of her influence on me. I always wanted to be good just for her.

But I didn't have the courage. I tried to accept that it was over.

I left without saying anything at all, and walked to my car with a new layer of grief inside. Except for once in passing, I would not see her again for nearly twenty years, and by then we were both different people.

After many years, I have concluded that the reason she made me feel confident at age fourteen and beyond was because she had the intellect and the emotional make-up of a mature, calm adult. She might have been the only one I knew who totally fit that description.

During our breakup and afterwards, I vowed to myself that I would try to be the person she thought I was.

If the emotional quagmire that first separated us presented itself to me today, I still would not know what the best decision would be, because now I realize that I did not know Julie; and she was right— she did not know me.

I denied her that.

Today, before and after occasional high school reunions, Julie and I can exchange emails and be distant friends, and that is fine with me, because I realize that after all these years she is a person I hardly know. Like me, I know she remembers the Julie she was when that Julie was mine, and we have that memory in common.

But the memories of those times are safe in a compartment separate from our current circumstances, as they should be.
I believe Julie came into my life for a purpose, and that purpose was fulfilled. Nancy Leach and Julie Richards inspired me to try to be what they thought I should be and what I wanted to be.

CHAPTER 11

LEAVING DAD AND HOME BEHIND

When I moved back to Odessa, a good friend connected me with a job at a local teen hangout.

I enrolled in Odessa College and agreed to live with my brother Butch and his wife, Kay, and their three young children. This was one of the poorer decisions I have ever made, but, in fact, they needed me. Their finances were always in crisis. They had just been evicted from a duplex for not paying rent, and I found a house where we could all live.

I agreed to pay every other month's rent while I lived with them, which would give them some financial relief, and for this reason, I thought things might work out. Since they were broke, it was my turn as soon as we moved in.

Butch worked in the oilfields on a midnight shift, and when he had to have a car, he drove mine, because their car had been repossessed. So I was working and going to college, carrying fifteen academic credit hours, and paying half the rent and furnishing the household's only car.

If Kay had owned King Solomon's mines, she still would have ended up a pauper. I don't think I ever knew a more foolish woman when it came to money. It seemed to slip away from her as easily as clouds blown by the wind, here one minute and gone the next.

At the end of the first month, Kay persuaded Butch that they ought to have my paycheck even though it was their turn to pay the rent. I had already fronted an entire month's existence to those two and their kids, but it was evidently not enough for them.

The morning after I was paid, I was abruptly awakened to find my brother sitting on my chest, pinning me under the covers and hitting me in the face with his fists, cursing about money. I managed to throw him off me, and, completely disoriented, it was all I could do to pull on a T-shirt and some jeans and get out to my car and leave, my nose bloodied and my eyes blackened and puffy.

After thirty minutes or so, I got my wits back and figured out what he had done and why. Were they both totally nuts?

I stormed back to the house wanting to fight. I pushed Butch, and cursed him, but didn't punch him. He just took it. He seemed to be ashamed, but said nothing.

I went to class and to work with my black eyes and bruised face, and if anyone asked me what happened, I told them. I didn't try to defend Butch in any way. I got a lot of silent, shocked looks that day.

Weeks later, when I unavoidably came across Butch, he sheepishly apologized.

I was ashamed that something so disgraceful had happened between us. That shame was a monkey on my back, one I still deal with.

***

I was back on the streets again.

An old friend, Cameron Ray, now married, took me in. He and Aline lived in a small, upstairs garage apartment, and they had an extra bedroom I could use. I stayed with them for a few months until I finally found a private room I could afford.

I had a place to sleep, but meals were another matter. My diet consisted of convenience store fare: a baked apple pie and a Coke for breakfast, a fast-food hamburger, French fries, and a Coke for lunch, and milk and peanut butter crackers for supper. It was not the healthiest diet, but it was all my small paycheck could handle.

After my fall semester at Tarleton, and in spite of my being a prime example of a poor, struggling student, attending Odessa College that spring seemed like heaven to me. It was something of a homecoming and a new start. I was pleasantly surprised to find a fairly large population of old friends from both sides of town, and even a few from my elementary school years at Notrees.

I felt at home.

A new, but at the same time familiar, group emerged as my circle of friends. Some had been distant acquaintances, and some knew me quite well. We came together as college students with a shared past, and it added up to a good time.

Sometimes I had too much fun, and my grades reflected that. I realize now, and probably knew then, that college was also an opportunity to experience a normal social life, something I had sorely missed in high school. The social life and my work hours made studying and doing homework difficult. I thought I could get by, but college demanded much more work than high school. I was disorganized and had no mentors. My grades would have been much better had I known how to plan better. But I did love college life; most importantly, I felt I was at last where I wanted to be, doing what I wanted to do, with people I wanted to do things with.

A huge weight lifted from me. My life was transitioning away from the embarrassments and entrapments of the past.

***

While the sharp edges of my family life were softening a bit, my dad was still in town and still affected my life at times. I had a part-time job and was feeling somewhat comfortable, but his life was a wreck.

Sometime during that first semester at Odessa College, someone dropped him off at my workplace.

I looked up when I heard him say, "Hey Mike! How are ya?"

Before I could answer, he continued: "I need a favor. I got a job and have to report tomorrow. Can you loan me fifteen dollars to get some gloves and work boots? I'll pay you back with my first check."

He had a happy grin on his face.

"Sure," I said, "but I close at ten p.m. Be here."

"No sweat, but I need your car for a few minutes. I want to run up to

Sears and Roebuck." I gave him my key and he left.

Ten o'clock, and then ten-thirty, came and went. I phoned Cameron and asked him to help me find my Chevy. My intuition led me to the Club Café in downtown Odessa, across from the courthouse.

I found my little Chevy. In the front seat, keeled over like a beached whale, was dear ol' Dad, drunker than a skunk, with two bottles of vodka on the floorboard, one empty and the other half-empty. There was no sign of new boots or gloves.

I had been conned again. He had lied all the way. He took my hard-earned money just to get drunk!

Wow! Did my dad blame me for everything bad that had happened to him? What had I ever done over the years to make him think so little of me that he would lie to con me out of my pitifully scarce money and do nothing but get drunk with it? He believed I was not his son, I guess, so anything goes. He had not a single ounce of integrity left in his soul.

I just looked at his unconscious figure and shook my head. I walked back to where Cameron waited in his car.

"It's him," I said. "Passed out. Can you believe this shit?"

Cameron just shook his head and smiled weakly.

Pissed off and disbelieving, I got into the driver's seat, pushed the drunk into a tighter pile, cranked the engine and headed toward his girlfriend's house to dump him. He sloshed awake and made a sloppy attempt at conversation.

Ignoring him, I reached into the back seat and retrieved the half-bottle of vodka, showed it to him, and held it out the window and dropped it on the pavement.

Eyes wide at the sound of his precious bottle breaking, he said, "You shouldn't have done that."

This drunk had balls, but the wrong kind—his rolled around loose in his head.

"If I buy it, I can damn well do with it what I please," I said.

All the other times that he had pulled something like this, I had felt abused, but I had always nursed the hope that maybe, just maybe, he had some care for my efforts to survive. That night I realized that not only was there no concern for me and my survival, my own father was more than willing to take whatever I had worked for just to fill his gut with alcohol!

Never had I ever heard or met a person more bizarre than the man I saw that night.

I seriously doubted my dad had ever loved anyone, because from my perspective he mistreated everyone in his circle. But no one caught any more disrespect from him than I did, not even my mother. I think that if the man had found me dying on the side of the road, all he would have cared about is how much money he could scrounge from my pocket.

***

That night was pivotal—an emotionally life changing event for me.

My mom had died, my grandparents had died and now, the last adult in my family, my dad, was essentially gone, too. He was alive, but he was not there for me, and I had to accept that fact.

In a way, this left another hole in my already perforated chest, but in another way, it allowed me to close his chapter, too. I couldn't survive with him. I had to move on without him. My emotional bank held zero trust in him.

I was through.

Several people knew I was a sucker for wanting to see them straighten out their lives. They knew that if they told me the right tale of woe they could get what I had. Around this same time, my brother Butch shamelessly came to me when I had nothing to spare. He had blown his share of our inheritance, and begged me to take some money out of my trust for him because he was broke.

Like a fool, I did.

I had to finish three semesters at Odessa College. It was my best option, but after that, I knew I had to get away. My brother was a leech, and my father was no father. He was a fake, and I was a sucker. Odessa was my father's home, not mine. I could not carry him or fix him, and I could not help him. Real fathers give, not take.

Dad had become a full-fledged taker, a parasite living for one purpose: his drunken self. He had no pride, no remorse, and no good feelings about me.

I wanted to be done with him.

***

On the first day of class at Odessa College in the fall of 1963, I was waiting for a psychology class to start when a striking, curly-haired blonde entered the auditorium.

My heart jumped—wow, who is that?

The girl next to me told me the beauty's name was Cheryl Lynn Parmer. The next day Cheryl happened to order lunch at the student union at the same time I did. I invited her to share a table, and soon we were seeing each other exclusively.

Although Cheryl and I were serious, at the end of the school year my brain still told me I needed to get the hell out of Odessa and away from the people and circumstances that held me back. Life was just too much of a soap opera for me in my home town. The summer after I completed my sophomore year at Odessa College, Cheryl agreed.

I needed to decide where to finish my degree. Two friends convinced me that there were many more jobs in Houston than in West Texas, and I could attend the University of Houston. Roger Rankin, Ken Hatch, and I packed our cars with all of our belongings and caravanned eastward toward a new life in the city.

None of us ever lived in Odessa again.

CHAPTER 12

MARRIAGE AND FLYING

When I went to Houston in the summer of 1964, I left my girlfriend Cheryl behind in Odessa.

I missed her terribly, and it was obvious from her frequent letters that she was also unhappy. In my letters I always told her how much I missed her, but I didn't think it would be fair to ask her to marry me, because I had so little to offer with respect to financial security and family support.

I had been in Houston only a couple of weeks when Cheryl flew to Houston to see me. She could stay only one night because of her work schedule, so my roommates moved things around so she could have one of the two bedrooms; I got the living room sofa.

I could hardly believe she was there. We went to a Mexican restaurant to get a bite to eat and talk privately. She made small talk about my job and so on, but I felt something was coming.

She looked at me and said, "I don't want us living apart like this, Mike. I want to get married."

 It was not a complete surprise.

She knew I loved her, but she also knew my situation, and I suspected she understood why I had never proposed. My firm hug answered her. Relief washed over me as I could finally believe that she loved me, too, and wanted to marry me.

My head swam with gratitude.

She wanted a ceremony in her church in Odessa at the end of August, a little over two months away. We decided that I would give notice at my job at a discount store and return to Odessa early in August to be there for the preparations. Feeling lucky and proud to be marrying the girl I loved, at the end of July I loaded my 1960 Chevrolet with everything I owned and made the eight-hour haul to Odessa.

I stayed with Cheryl's family before the wedding. I sold Cutco knives to some friends to earn a little money, and slept on the living room couch at night. Cheryl's mom liked me, I could tell, and I got along with her sister and two younger brothers. Her father was skeptical, though, and that never changed.

Alford Smallwood should have been my best man. He was my best friend, but I knew Alford knew all my secrets and would understand my thinking: I didn't want my father around, my sister Lea was struggling financially in Dallas, and I didn't know where Shirley was. Including Alford would have connected me to them.

Instead, I asked my brother Butch to be my best man, not because I thought he was, but because I had no other family attending. Several of my friends sat on the groom's side, however, including Alford and his family, and Willie Beth Ray, the earthly angel who had helped me buy a car at one of my lowest points.

Among those in the pews was an Odessa College classmate. Cheryl and I knew him in passing, but neither of us knew his name; he had shown up uninvited. Evidently he had nursed a crush on Cheryl from a distance. He sat stiffly upright during the ceremony, his face oozing anguish. I was afraid he might drop dead from unmitigated grief right there in the church. He stood out from the happy crowd like a carbuncle sprouting from the nose of a beautiful friend. He did not attend the reception.

Just like that, in late August 1964, at the age of twenty-one, I became a married man.

Cheryl was just a few days from turning nineteen. After a wedding night in nearby Midland, we drove back to Odessa and packed our things in my car, said our good-byes, and headed to Houston.

We never lived in Odessa again. Cheryl never met my father, and that was fine with me.

***

Blonde and bubbly, Cheryl was not just good-looking, but a real head-turner. Her face wore a perpetual smile. She came from a stable family, and I felt fortunate to have snagged her for my wife. Our plan was to live in Houston and get jobs while I took night courses toward a degree in psychology at the University of Houston.

In order to accumulate a financial cushion, I delayed school for a year and worked as a manager trainee for J.C. Penney Department Stores in a shopping center not far from our little apartment on the Gulf Freeway. Cheryl worked in a men's shop, but quickly moved to a job with Emery Air Freight at nearby Hobby Airport. After learning about aviation, she took a job as a reservation agent for Trans Texas Airways at Hobby, a job she enjoyed and that gave us both a glimpse into the airline world.

Her office adjoined the flight dispatcher's office, where highly intelligent men kept track of every move that Trans Texas airliners made while en route all over Texas.

I met some of them, and a seed was planted in my brain.

Working for Trans Texas Airways had its benefits: all employees and spouses were given eight free flight passes a year. That was when flying was expensive, so those passes were much appreciated.

After our first year in Houston, I enrolled again at the University of Houston. I lacked confidence to the point it pained me. I was interested in clinical psychology, thinking it would help me to better understand myself and my family and the dysfunction that dogged us. I hoped to become someone unafraid of my abilities. I was sorely disappointed to find that the field of psychology doesn't address changing oneself, even today.

An experimental psychology course gave me a look at what a clinical psychologist did for a living, and I became disillusioned. At that time, the field was dominated by the behaviorists who wrote the textbooks. I thought their goals were so narrow as to be ineffective.

I got discouraged about my career choices, and that launched me into a state of semi-depression. I had no idea who or what I wanted to be when I grew up.

Cheryl saw the change and I knew she was disappointed in me. I was so lost that the rest of my courses suffered, too. I tried getting interested in history and literature as majors, but did not anticipate a happy future teaching school.

By the spring of 1966, my college transcript was awful, and I felt like a failure.

***

A conversation with my sister Shirley changed everything.

Shirley had married a bright guy named Bob Calloway, a high school football player of college caliber and her high school sweetheart in Monahans. I lost track of them after they eloped, and then one day out of the blue a letter came from Shirley. I was surprised to learn that Bob was now a commercial pilot instructing Air Force students in Laredo.

I called Shirley to find out more. She told me that Bob had learned of the job opportunity and had borrowed enough money to get his licenses, which he did in just ninety days at the Amarillo airport, knowing he could repay the loan with the new job.

She also said they did not like Laredo and were approved for a transfer to Big Spring, where Webb Air Force base offered the same training program at the nearby civilian Howard County Airport. Big Spring was much closer to Bob's hometown of Monahans, and only sixty miles east of Odessa, and they were packing for the move at the very time I called.

Then Shirley said some magic words: "I'm sure Bob would teach you to fly for free if you come to Big Spring."

I jumped at the opportunity. Cheryl agreed that I should do it. It took me about five minutes after the semester ended to pack.

The trouble was that we had no money.

Cheryl called her parents, but they were not well off at the time and declined to help. I called Bob Calloway, and we talked and crunched the numbers. We concluded that nine hundred dollars would do it, and Cheryl and I thought we had that much coming back on an income tax return, so I went to Big Spring to stay with Bob and

Shirley. Cheryl stayed in Houston to give notice at her job and save some money, too. I hated to leave her behind, but we both knew it was for our future.

Using one of our Trans Texas passes, I flew to back to West Texas. Bob met me at the Midland-Odessa airport just as night was falling on an early June evening. My old home town was just ten miles to the west. My new home base would be Big Spring, forty miles to the east. I reveled in the cool desert breeze as I took in the runway lights, the threshold and taxiway lights, the rotating beacon, and the dark silhouettes of idle airplanes.

It was close to heaven.

Bob had flown the Piper Tri-Pacer from Big Spring to get me—the same plane I would learn to fly—and had gotten permission from the control tower to park at the same gate as the Trans Texas Airways fifty-passenger Convair 240 that I had ridden in from Houston. We loaded my trunk into the back seat of the Tri-Pacer and strapped ourselves into the cockpit as the two pilots of the TTA Convair beside us watched in curiosity.

I detected scents of warm metal, oil, fabric, leather, and canvas. There is no telling how much sweat was blended into all that, and I wondered what else there might be. My first two hundred hours of flying time were in that airplane, and the look and feel and smells of that cockpit are with me still. Bob systematically went through a memorized checklist as he fired up the engine and flipped switches that brought the glowing panel lights to life.

I could not have been more thrilled as I listened to the radio transmissions between my new instructor and the control tower, knowing I was at the beginning of a new life's adventure. I thought of Cheryl, back in Houston, earning a sparse living for us. I did not want to disappoint her.

Bob and I reached the beginning of an active runway; he completed the engine run-up and told the tower we were ready for take-off. After the tower cleared us, Bob lined us up on the runaway and applied full throttle. The airplane shuddered to a full roar, shook like a wet dog, smoothed out, and rolled forward at ever-increasing speed.

The real magic began as we lifted off in a slightly nose-up attitude and fled the earth into the inky-black night sky.

I could see the lights of Odessa to my right. I looked for the dark cemetery on its outskirts, where six short years earlier my mother had been buried, leaving her bewildered kids behind. I still knew many people from those days, but two years had passed since I left, and my memories were fading, just as the others carried on with their own lives.

I wondered if my hopelessly homeless father was down there somewhere, bumming around near one of those thousands of lights.

Still climbing, we turned east toward Midland, which was at our nine o'clock position. I looked down at Highway 80, which I had traveled a mind-numbing number of times, and marveled that now I was soaring high above it. I wondered if any of those cars carried people I knew. If so, I silently thought maybe they'd be surprised to know that I, Mike Moore, was high above them.

Would they want to know that I was headed to a completely new life?

Like Bob, sitting next to me in the left seat, I, too, would have Air Force students, first in front of me at a desk and then beside me in a cockpit. I would teach them how to fly airplanes similar to the one Bob and I were in right now.

Later, those young pilots would go on to an Air Force instructor who would teach them about jets. They would eventually fly over Southeast Asia in a bloody war, and would be a part of history that we would read about forever.

I would have been the one who introduced them to the air, and they would someday remember who first taught them to fly, and they, too, would think of it all as a great adventure, a privilege to slip those surly bonds of earth and be like a bird—way more than a bird.

How spectacular can life get?

We leveled off at cruising altitude toward Big Spring. Bob skillfully maneuvered our airplane below the intense night jet traffic at Webb Air Force Base and we continued toward the traffic pattern at nearby Howard County Airport.

I saw the rotating beacon and watched intently as my instructor went through his checks and changes in power; he turned us multiple times until the runway was right in front of us, waiting, illuminated by our landing light. The airport was peacefully quiet. We touched down gently, and Bob turned onto the taxiway and then finally onto the parking ramp beside the USAF hanger and mobile control tower. About thirty USAF T-41s were parked on the ramp—a glimpse of my future.

We disembarked, and for a quick, private moment I stood in the darkness and put my hand on the little plane like it was alive, with a spirit. I wanted to be its friend. I silently thanked it, marveling at the night world of tethered airplanes around me.

I quietly thanked God that I was allowed to embark on this new adventure.

***

The next day, Bob and I went to a bank and explained Cheryl's and my coming tax refund of nine hundred dollars. The banker let me pledge that refund for collateral for a loan that would get me my licenses.

I had my first lesson with Bob that afternoon.

After a couple of weeks, I completed a fairly uneventful solo in the traffic pattern, and started to believe I could really do this. My next assignment was to fly by myself to a practice area where I would start honing my skills with flight maneuvers such as stalls, slow flight, forced landings, and so on without the benefit and security of my instructor beside me.

No student pilot ever forgets his or her first solo away from the airport. I was not afraid, but maybe I should have been.

I probably spent more time contemplating the maneuvers than actually practicing them. I remember getting airborne after an exhaustive pre-flight inspection of that older Piper Tri-Pacer.

I flew away from the busy Big Spring civilian airport and transitioned to the practice areas to the northeast near the Snyder, Texas airport. I told myself to fly the limits of the practice area to make sure there were no intruders such as other airplanes, vultures, hawks, butterflies, or anything that might stray into my windshield.

I looked it all over with all the vigilance I could muster. The T-41 program at the Howard County airport was as busy as a hornet's nest at times, and I knew I was just on the edge of the military practice areas; it was just one more thing to worry about.

I was also putting off the stalls and other maneuvers as long as possible.

Finally, I tried a few quick stalls, or maybe they were just approaches to stalls! I tried slow flying with an unnecessarily high and comfortable margin of error. No sense in being stupid the first time out, right? I talked to myself a lot as a student pilot, which was a way for me to focus.

Let's see, what else is there to practice? Level turns? I did those while scouting the area. *Coordinated turns?* They take only seconds and were not too exciting, anyway.

After a long ten minutes of cautiously executed maneuvers, I decided it must be time to head back and maybe, just maybe, I would practice touch-and-go landings in the airport traffic pattern. No sense in staying out here too long and worrying everybody. That would be selfish, and I didn't want anyone accusing me of being thoughtless.

Let's mosey back and keep the world happy. Yeah!

Set the navigational instrument to the Big Spring VOR for a southwest heading back to HCA airport. Level off checklist! Everything is cool.

In fifteen minutes or so, I completed the descent. I approached the traffic pattern at a forty-five degree angle to a left downwind for Runway 16. I visually cleared for traffic, telling myself to be vigilant in scanning the airspace. I crosschecked my flight instruments, called Unicom, and announced my position and intentions.

Check. I made the turn to downwind. Check.

But something is wrong—bad wrong.

The hair on my arms is standing up. I'm breathing too hard. What is it? I feel a deep foreboding and I have no idea why. I double-check everything I can as I rapidly approach my left base-leg turn.

Warning bells clanged in my head. Why? *Look! Look everywhere!*

I announce my turn to left base on the radio. Adjust airspeed, I'm too fast. A Tri-Pacer is a brick, slowing rapidly.

Careful, don't overshoot, keep the throttle in, and keep banking. It's okay. You're a little hot, but what the hell—you're flying a canvas brick!

So what could be wrong? Near panic, I continue talking to myself.

A voice inside my head coaxed me, Calm down. No! Look below—dip the nose and slip it down. Now!

I maneuver into a downward, cross-controlled slip and look to see what is below me. Out of seemingly nowhere, I spot a light, twin-engine Piper Aztec barely beneath me, starting his flare for a landing on the rapidly approaching runway. Had I not looked, I would have descended into his propellers.

Where the hell did he come from?

I hit full left rudder. I hit full throttle, hard, fast. *Too fast—the engine quit!*

I had flooded the engine with too much fuel, too fast. With no engine power, the cockpit is sickeningly quiet. I barely missed the Aztec, but now I am headed toward the rough, wild terrain on the side of the runway.

I must flare to make contact with the ground that is rushing up at me. As I pull back on the controls, the airplane crunches onto the short strip of grass next to the runway. I leave the grass and start hitting bumpy ground. I am at an angle, headed toward the choppy desert terrain.

Luckily, I've held the nose wheel up. The other airplane is completely unaware of our near miss.

Meanwhile, I am fighting for my life.

The engine kicks in at full throttle. Still in a nose-up attitude, the airplane accelerates, catapulting through tall grass and cactus and uneven dirt. I hear and feel a hard bump a microsecond before I leave the ground again at full power.

I'm airborne again!

Now I know I won't have to survive a sudden stop in the unforgiving desert terrain, trapped upside down in a burning airplane. I have just dodged a huge bullet. But I must nurse this baby back into the sky without stalling.

I have my hands full as I focus on what I've broken. *Have I beat up the airplane too much to make a safe landing?* Is my nose wheel damaged, or gone?

I'm still in a shallow climb, fast and safe for the moment. I reach a safe altitude and level off. I am probably eight miles from the field. I breathe easier.

I must reverse course.

I descend again to traffic pattern altitude. *What next? Did I make a radio call?*

I announce my position and intent to any monitoring traffic around the uncontrolled airport. I desperately want this airplane back on the ground safely without being a spectacle! Part of me feels peaceful and safe, yet the adrenaline surges.

Once more I come in for a landing, this time with too much airspeed, sensing that I will be better off a bit fast than too slow. Anxious, but with no voices inside my head screaming at me this time, I feel the main tires chirp onto the asphalt in a smooth landing.

I hold the nose wheel off the runway as long as it will stay up, but it eventually settles and I know something is wrong. Slowly, gently, I apply the hand brakes.

Gosh, the nose wheel is wobbly! The throttle knob's shaft in my right hand is bent downward. *How on earth?*

My roll across the rough terrain broke the motor mounts. At least the nose wheel was still intact. Clearing the active runway, I must have advanced the throttle for my go-around with so much force that I bent the stainless steel throttle rod.

I cursed myself. Self-doubt enveloped me like black smoke.

Several people witnessed my near disaster. Most were military personnel with the T-41 program, but a couple were grim-faced civilian instructors.

Why didn't I see that Aztec? Hell, I could have been turned into hamburger meat for the buzzards.

Shaking, I went over each item on the shutdown checklist.

Just then my instructor brother-in-law showed up.

"Hey!" he said. "I hear you had one hell of a landing! Let me buy you a beer."

We went to the raucous officers' club at Webb Air Force Base to wind down, along with hundreds of other Air Force students and instructors loudly celebrating the end of a tough day. None had had a day like mine—of that I was sure.

I was soon told that the Aztec pilot had made an unannounced, illegal, long, low, straight-in approach to a busy, uncontrolled airfield and almost got us both killed. He was severely reprimanded by both the local military officers and the FAA.

My intuition had saved both our lives.

One old-timer, a revered T-41 flight instructor and former

barnstormer, told me I "did a hell of a good job of flying the airplane out of trouble." I'll never forget that. Thank you, Eddie.

Like an aspiring cowboy who got bucked off his horse, I climbed back into the cockpit as soon as the Tri-Pacer was repaired—about three days. I figured that since I had survived, it must be a sign this was meant to be, and I pressed on.

Never have I had such a strong, silent warning invade my consciousness so dramatically. Never before did I need it more, I guess, and as I write this, in my late seventies, I still wonder how it all worked. I thank my Creator every time the memory pops up.

*   *   *

Cheryl joined me in Big Spring at the end of the summer. We lived with my sister Shirley and her family while I finished my training. I was glad to have her around again.

Studying for my aviation exams taught me that learning the matter at hand requires complete immersion in the subject—no exceptions. I wished that truth had come to me when I was in high school!

I completed the certification requirements for my commercial pilot's license and flight instructor rating in mid-November.

Through the military contacts I made at the Big Spring T-41 program, I got my first T-41 instructor's job at the municipal airport in Del Rio, not far from the USAF jet training program at Laughlin Air Force Base. Even though I had no instructing experience, demand for pilots was so high that even inexperienced guys like me were needed.

I flew four training missions a day, five days a week, building time and experience.

The Air Force flight training program was clearly presented and very effective in screening new pilots. The program instilled in me a highly disciplined approach that has carried over to other areas of my life. (I am a checklist freak to this day.) My students were all college graduates and highly motivated, and I am proud to know that I had a part in training a group I think of as America's best.

I loved the job. I now knew what I wanted to be when I grew up—an airline pilot!

I wanted to be in larger city to develop more contacts, so after a year in Del Rio, Cheryl and I moved to Lubbock, where there was an opening at the Lubbock Municipal Airport with the T-41 program in conjunction with nearby Reese Air Force Base.

I thought Cheryl might take advantage of the opportunity to take some courses at Texas Tech University towards her unfinished degree, although she never did.
I eventually concluded that all the airline pilot jobs were going to the huge number of jet pilots getting out of the military. A civilian pilot had no chance.

It was nuts. For lack of a college degree, I could not get into the Air Force as a pilot; I could train them, but I could not be one of them, even though I had a signed letter from an Air Force major saying I was capable of soloing the T-37 jet after my very first flight in one. I got to fly that jet trainer twice and I experienced a burst of euphoria the first time I took it off and did aileron rolls like Willard Van Brunt did over Notrees when I was ten years old. Those two jet flights were an incredible thrill. Few civilians get that privilege.

Early in 1968, I decided to try to get into the Texas Air National Guard.

I flew to Houston and weaseled my way into the base commander's office at Ellington Air Force Base. I had something better than an appointment: a sneaky plan. I walked into the reception area with a feigned sense of importance and told the secretary that I was there to see the colonel, as if he were expecting me. I was ushered into his office where I introduced myself, shook his hand, and sat down across from him without being invited to do so.

I wanted to be brash.

Surprised that I got by his secretary so easily, the full bird colonel listened as I expressed my desire to fly for the Texas Air National Guard.

"Son, that takes ultra-strong political influence during war time," he said.
When I told him that the former Attorney General of the State of Texas would vouch for me, he chuckled softly.

"The last guy to get into the Air Guard that I know of had a father with strong connections in the CIA."

I didn't bring up my dad, the bankrupt alcoholic. I gave the colonel a copy of the letter about my capabilities in the T-37 jet and continued to make my case.

He scanned the letter and then handed it back and wished me luck.

I thanked him and left. Still faking self-importance, I nodded at the suspicious secretary as I walked past her. I would love to have heard the exchange between her and her boss after I left.

Rejected and dejected, I went back to Lubbock.

***

During our time in Lubbock, a neighbor in our apartment complex asked Cheryl to work some evenings as a greeter at The Embers Steakhouse, the nicest restaurant in town in the late sixties.

One evening when she was not working, we were at happy hour there with friends. A young guy at the bar watched us, ogling Cheryl while pounding down drinks. He got so smashed that he staggered over and kissed her smack on the mouth.

She jerked loose and laughed but was clearly shocked. I gave the creep a look that told him he had better get out of Dodge, fast. The owner, Cheryl's boss, quickly escorted the drunk to the door. There was a popular song in the sixties about the pains of marrying a beautiful woman.

I knew that truth.

By this time, we were definitely past the honeymoon stage. Cheryl had grown disillusioned with me in Houston when my grades slipped as I searched for another future.

I believe she thought I didn't try hard enough in many areas, and I have to admit she was probably right. I can see my subconscious reasoning now: if I tried my best and failed, it would prove I wasn't good enough; but if I didn't give it my all and it didn't work out, I could reason that I simply hadn't worked hard enough. My frustration with myself compounded the problem.

We bickered over trivial things. In nearly all our time together, Cheryl and I never argued, but that changed in Lubbock when all the glue started to come loose from our marriage.

She confided to her mother that she didn't think I could take care of her emotionally or financially, and her mother relayed that to me. That really hurt, but I knew I had it coming. I had the same suspicions.

Cheryl was frequently hit on because of her looks, and I wondered if she was attracted to the flight instructor we had met in Del Rio. I had seen the sparks fly between them, and he had also moved to Lubbock, his home town.

Were they seeing each other? The suspicion ate at me and eventually manifested in a diagnosis of ulcerative colitis—internal bleeding. And that meant I couldn't be a pilot if I revealed that to the FAA at my next flight physical. I kept my mouth shut and continued my flight instructing job while looking for other career options.

I didn't tell Cheryl because I knew she would see it as another failure. Maybe she was right—I didn't have the right stuff. The medication and bland diet compounded my desperation to find a clear path to something better.

Depression hung over me.

One Saturday when Cheryl was at work, I lay down on the sofa and closed my eyes and reasoned with myself about what was happening.

I admitted that I had to go on, no matter what—but that I also had to change things.

I couldn't let myself, or Cheryl, destroy my health. I concluded that with or without a marriage, and with or without a clear career path, I had to survive.

I also knew I had be kinder to myself. Taking deep breaths and slowly letting them out, I allowed myself to relax, knowing I would go on, come what may.

I actually felt a release and an amazing sensation of healing in my stomach. Was it possible that my ulcerative colitis was purely a stress response?

The condition seemed to heal itself when I relaxed and accepted my situation. The bleeding stopped over the next few days and never recurred, although I knew it could. I said nothing to anyone, because I feared it wasn't true and that no one would believe it. I also knew that my flying days were over if I told the truth.

I kept talking to myself, convincing myself to let things go and simply accept whatever happened.

I sensed I was healed, but also realized that if I couldn't have a flying career, I had to find another way to make a living. The thought of flying my own airplane buoyed me, but my outlook remained uncertain as Cheryl slipped away from me.

***

Cheryl was a bit tipsy when she came home late one night from her job, which was completely unlike her. I thought she was feeling frisky, and was encouraged that maybe we had turned a corner.

"I love you," she told me while we were in bed. "I will always love you. No matter what happens. I hope you believe that."

I remember thinking I should keep some vodka on hand for her. But I was a fool again. I later realized that she was really telling me good-bye.

I did not want to have to admit to another career failure, and I thought about finding a job as an aircraft dispatcher. I could get to know the lay of the land that way, and perhaps make contacts and work my way into a co-pilot's seat.

While most people know what a pilot does, few are aware that dispatchers even exist.

In a nutshell, dispatchers are "the heart of the airline." They share legal responsibility for the flight with the captain of the airplane. It is the dispatcher's job to "release" each flight and make sure the flight crews have all the information they need to conduct the flight within industry regulations.

The dispatcher chooses which alternate airports a given flight is to use in the event of bad weather at the destination; in the days before computers, dispatchers also calculated fuel loads and take-off weights for each leg of an airplane's route, taking into consideration how many passengers were on board at each stop. It is the aircraft dispatcher's responsibility to provide updates on changes in the weather and at the airport (such as icy or disabled runways), and much more. The dispatch office also focuses on profitability, keeping track of fuel prices and other operational costs.

I started scanning the Lubbock newspaper ads, and one day saw an ad for an aircraft dispatcher's job with Frontier Airlines in Denver, Colorado. I applied, and Cheryl and I drove to Denver for the interview.

The position required a dispatcher's license, but based on my credentials, I was hired as an assistant dispatcher, with the provision that I would get licensed within two years.

The written exam is notoriously difficult. I was told of a Frontier captain who had been a lawyer and who claimed the airline transport pilot's exam was harder than the bar exam.

The airline dispatcher's test covers the airline transport pilot's body of knowledge plus the laws and regulations that apply only to dispatchers.

Being a dispatcher is not easy, but it is an honorable career and over time commands a decent paycheck. In addition, as airline employees, dispatchers enjoy free or reduced fare flight privileges—a big hook.

I was relieved and excited at the prospect of a new start.

I was supposed to report for work in thirty days, so I subscribed to the Denver newspaper to find a place to live. I found an option that seemed promising and pointed it out to Cheryl.

She shook her head no without even looking at me.

"I'm going home to my folks, Mike," she said. "We have to get a divorce."

She had clearly pondered the situation for a long time. She was a loyal, good wife to my knowledge; I had complete faith in her and her upbringing. I was a loyal husband, but the marriage did not work, and it was my fault.

The cold, hard truth is that she hated my self-doubt. My lack of confidence drove her away. She was a bright, hard-charging adventurer who thought she could do anything, and could not understand why I was so lacking.

I never blamed her.

What drove her away was the baggage of my upbringing, the details of which she never fully knew. I hid my past to prevent her from sprinting away like Julie Richards had.

The fault was mine. I didn't know how to deal with the truth and shame that seemed to push others away.

Our parting was amicable, with no children and few belongings to argue over, but we could not remain friends. I cared too deeply.

Letting each other go completely was best.

With another hole in my chest, I pulled a U-Haul trailer to Denver, alone, in April 1968.

CHAPTER 13

RECOGNIZING AND EMBRACING THE TRUTH

It was crying time again.

I was grieving. I didn't know a soul in Denver and had no friends or family anywhere nearby—no support group at all.

I had not anticipated that the job at Frontier had rotating shifts, and my body never adjusted to a regular routine or established healthy sleep patterns.

I worked four days on the day shift (seven a.m. to three p.m.), then two days off followed by the midnight shift (eleven p.m. to seven a.m.), then two days off followed by a swing shift (three p.m. to eleven p.m.), with two days off before starting the cycle again. I had Saturday-Sunday weekends only every six weeks.

The work was exhilarating but hectic. It was non-stop answering telephones and keeping track of flights and supplying crews with weather and airport information. Bad weather made the workload worse than hell. We had no lunch or coffee breaks; lunch was from a brown bag I packed myself, eaten quickly at my desk or it was a quick sandwich from a vending machine down the hallway.

As a unionized new hire, I was at the bottom of the seniority ladder, years away from making a good living. I started to wonder if I had made another mistake.

Outside of work, I was by myself most of the time. I kept my feelings tightly bottled up at work and made some good friends, but I let the loss of Cheryl consume me when I was alone.

When the divorce was final in August, Cheryl and her parents came to Denver to collect her share of our meager belongings.

I assumed we'd talk and she assured me we would. I still had a faint hope of reconciliation, but she had no interest, and her father was hostile to me in my own apartment, as if he owned it.

He tried to shove me out my own door so they could take what they wanted. I was disgusted but let them take whatever they chose to take.

I never talked to any of them again.

***

By September I did not like the thoughts that were filling my mind. Scariest was the sense that I didn't care if I died.

Nothing seemed to matter. To hell with survival, much less ambition.

I had the attitude of a victim and didn't want to fight anymore. I had failed with both Julie and Cheryl. I knew I was the cause, but I could not understand why it happened.

Several women had hit on me, but none did anything for me. I was scared to death of women in spite of being so fascinated with them. These new women were nothing compared to Cheryl, so what the hell was the point, if relationships only meant failure?

Most of all, I was sick and tired of not having any confidence—of comparing myself to others and always coming out so damn poor and alone.

Ending it all at twenty-five made perfect sense.

I was deeply depressed again—but this time I recognized the symptoms.

I made an appointment with a psychiatrist, but he seemed to me to have no self-confidence either. After a couple of sessions, he directed me to an occupational therapist.

Her office was on the third floor and had a lot of windows. One day, we were looking out at the trees with red and yellow leaves that signaled a beautiful Rocky Mountain autumn. The scene was a sharp contrast to my mood, which was as dark as the inside of a cave.

"Mike," she said. "We have talked twice before. I want to hear from you again why you think you're here."

"Because I am miserable," I told her. "I've lost everything I've fought for to get a normal life."

She shook her head. I waited.

"But what I haven't heard you say is that you have always bottled up your emotions, and that you never told the women in your life how much you cared for them. You've got to learn to share yourself and be more open. You expect women to read your mind, and that's not how it works."

I felt like she was probing every dark recess of my mind.

"I was protecting them," I said.

She shook her head again. "I'm not sure I buy that. I think you told them just enough to make them feel sorry for you—that was how you brought them into your life."

I placed all my victim cards on the table. "You don't know everything I went through."

She paused, looking at me with her head almost sideways, squinting doubtfully, and then threw her best punch.

"Poor you. Poor you. Poor you! That's baloney, Mike." She smiled like an arrogant Cheshire cat and shook her head in disgust. "Poor you. Poor you. Poor you."

My whole adult life flashed by as nothing but a pity party.

Truth exploded inside me. I held up my hand to silence her and I told her to hush.

Her face acknowledged my rudeness but she did not respond. She seemed to see something happening inside me.

It all clicked. I was getting it! It was a truth bath with a firehose, and it exposed the precious lies I told myself about being a victim.

I felt the truth of her words.

Weight left my shoulders. The room brightened, and then the world beyond.

It's one thing to hear the old proverb about truth setting you free, but it is an entirely different thing to experience it and truly know it.

I had dwelled in a state of self-pity and victimhood. The therapist revealed within me the answers I had searched for most of my life.

In one explosive moment, I realized that I always held back, fearing my best would never be good enough. I understood that survival is more than just getting from one day to the next. The inner self I had lived with was not the true me. I would get to know my true self only if I gave things my best and attacked my weaknesses until they became strengths.

The fog was clearing. I didn't need to be a manipulator. If others could succeed without manipulation, so could I!

I understood why the girls I loved left me. A woman can't trust you to take care of her if you don't think you can even take care of yourself.

Sorry, Nancy, Julie, and Cheryl. I wasted your time.

My whole life passed before me through a new perspective.

Life would change only when I changed. Just as I felt the ulcerative colitis heal when I relaxed and accepted my fate, I now felt the old Mike leave, a ghost finally finding the peace needed to move on.

In the most dramatic moment of my life, I vowed that no matter what path I chose, I was going to give it my best and let the chips fall where they may. Even failure was beneficial, a stepping stone.

I apologized to the therapist for my rudeness and left feeling like a new person, one filled with gusto.

* * *

Several co-workers commented on the difference in me. It was a noticeable change, and it felt good.

I decided I wanted to pass the aircraft dispatcher's written and oral exams, whether or not I chose to stay with the job I had. I didn't want to quit just because it was hard.

I sometimes jogged in a park that had a magnificent view of the Rockies. The mountains magically changed from one day to the next with an aspen show, or a snow show, or a cloud show.

I felt my own changes happening within me as fall turned to winter. I knew I wanted a profession where I determined my own income potential—and I wanted my own dad-gum airplane.

This meant rethinking my whole perspective about earning a living.

CHAPTER 14

ANOTHER SHOT AT ROMANCE

Christmas in 1968 fell on a cold Wednesday. I finished my midnight shift and slept about three hours, then got up.

Sacrificing a bit of sleep was worth it. I had been invited to a noon Christmas party in the apartment across the hall.

Spending the holiday with acquaintances filled me with cautious anticipation. Being alone was a first for me, and it felt strange. I was not in contact with my dad, brother, or sisters, and wondered where they were. I pushed back a deep sadness and silently wished them well, no matter what.

Cheryl crossed my mind but that relationship was over, and I realized that I could think of her without regret.

I wondered if things could get worse in our divided country. War was raging in Southeast Asia, and airports were full of men in uniform. Closer to home, protesters and civil rights activists were rioting and burning their own cities.

I had been drafted for Vietnam, but flunked the physical because of my bout with ulcerative colitis. My commercial flying ambitions were dead for now.

But other aspects of life were good—almost miraculous.

***

Six months earlier, when I got my first full paycheck, I spent a

Saturday morning searching for an apartment. I walked from building to building and came upon one on Capitol Hill near downtown. It had a sign that read "Efficiency Apartments." The address was 727 Pearl Street.

The number of my favorite Boeing airliner.

None of the buildings I had passed displayed a vacancy sign, including this one, but I knocked anyway.

I entered the lobby and pushed the intercom button that said Manager. Almost immediately, a woman in her fifties, petite and with an impish smile, emerged from down the hallway. Her name tag said she was Mrs. Klock, Manager.

She asked what I wanted, and I said an efficiency apartment.

She asked if I had a spot on the two-year waiting list.

"No, ma'am," I said, "but I thought I'd ask anyway."

She studied me for a moment, then said, "You're from Texas, aren't you?"

"Yes, ma'am."

"Follow me."

She said nothing as the elevator climbed to the sixth floor, shaking as the doors slid open. I followed Mrs. Klock down the hall to unit 605. She used one of the keys on her large keyring to open the door, and I followed her in.

Sunlight flooded the room as she opened the curtains on the sliding glass doors.

"This unit became available this morning," she said. "It's a hundred and twelve dollars a month, plus electricity. You can have it if you want it, but you have to decide right this minute."

Hardly believing my luck, I told her I would take it and would be back in thirty minutes, checkbook in hand.

As I headed back to the room I was renting, my heart pumped hard with the enormity of what had just transpired. Within the hour, I had a place to call my own.

As it happened, Mrs. Klock grew up on the Frio River in the Hill Country of Texas. I think she like my accent.

I moved in that afternoon and went to the nearby Safeway store and stocked the half-sized fridge in the closet-sized kitchen. Milk and peanut butter sandwich in hand, I opened the sliding glass door to my balcony and luxuriated in the briskness that is Denver, Colorado, as the sun slid behind the mountains.

I knew I was lucky. I felt myself relax as a layer of stress peeled off my body.

***

As I unpacked the next day, my neighbor from across the hall, Dave Coats, stopped by and introduced himself. He spotted two bottles of Jack Daniel's Tennessee sour mash bourbon on a countertop, gifts from my students, and offered to fix us both a drink.

He was in his thirties, athletic looking with a barrel chest, and acted very sure of himself. He told me he was from New Jersey and came to Denver on a ski trip and never went back. Recently divorced with two young daughters, he worked in advertising.

The more we chatted, the more I realized he and I were from very different cultures. A few days later, Dave invited me to his apartment to continue to get to know one another. Somehow I never saw those liquor bottles again after our first visit, but I didn't challenge him about it. This time, I had no liquor to offer.

It was May 1968. A cool breeze flowed through his balcony door and across the hall through my open balcony door. From Dave's balcony, Pike's Peak was visible ninety miles to the south.

Suddenly, there was a rustling, and maybe a giggle, outside his door. Like wolves, our ears went up. When Dave opened the door, three exceptionally well dressed, attractive ladies stood there, all about my age and all carrying grocery sacks.

Dave introduced me as the new guy from Texas and explained that they lived in the penthouse. I just nodded at them.

The older one of the group was Joan Parks, and there was Mary Alice Billingham, and beside her was a brunette named Janice. David thought of himself as a gourmet cook, and they were there to get a recipe. Joan copied the recipe as we all politely glanced back and forth at each other and made small talk.

Joan spoke with a familiar accent and all of them exuded Dallas class.

"Where are you ladies from?" I asked.

With a soft drawl, Joan replied, "Knoxville, Tennessee."

You could have knocked me over. I never knew folks from Tennessee sounded so much like us Texans, but I remembered Davy Crockett and his Tennessee volunteers and wondered if that was the source.

I could tell they were about to leave, so I spoke up: "Nice to meet you ladies. I think you all should come down some afternoon for a drink."

Joan quipped, "A drink of what?"

"Why, Tennessee sour mash, of course!"

We all laughed and they bustled out as quickly as they had bustled in, and I swear I heard whispers and a giggle before the elevator swallowed them up.

Dave and I stood staring at the empty doorway, and then he said as though talking to himself, "Those are some classy broads." Common ground between us, at last!

***

Christmas Day was the next time we all gathered again.

The air was electric. The United States and the world celebrated the successful Apollo 8 mission.

Everyone was excited. We understood that it was a precursor to landing men on the moon. Amidst the troubling riots and protests about the Vietnam War, the nation paused. For a few hours on that Christmas Day, our great country was unified.

Dave asked us to bring dishes to share, and I brought two bottles of wine and a Vicki Carr album. We became friends sharing Christmas Day away from home as we ate and sipped wine and watched the spectacular Apollo 8 mission on the muted TV, then danced to Vicki Carr.

Although most of the building's tenants were single working women, most brought a date, so the mix of sexes was fairly even. I sat on a barstool and watched a cute little lady I had never seen before as she brazenly flirted and danced with nearly every guy in the room. A sinfully low-cut dress revealed her perfect, apple-sized breasts. She'd had more than her share of wine and was quite aware that she was the center of attention.

She never looked my way.

A lustful thought or two registered in my sleepy brain, but I was content to just enjoy the scene as she danced a few feet away. The crowd soon made the room warm, and I grew sleepier.

I sipped my wine and considered asking Miss Apples to dance, just to see what would happen. Maybe she would wake me up.

The afternoon was fading, but I was patient. Finally she took a break, and emboldened by alcohol, I stood up to make my move.

I took two steps toward Miss Apples when I felt a tap on my shoulder. I turned around and stopped dead in my tracks.

It was Joan Parks, from Knoxville, Tennessee. The penthouse lady.

"I want to tell you something," she whispered as she leaned toward me, her hand cupping my ear.

I was stunned.

She took my hand and led me just inside Dave's bedroom. The door was open and we were in full view of most of the crowd as she moved closer.

She told me never to tell anyone what she said, so I won't, but it was so extraordinary that I wondered where this was going.

It finally dawned on my wine-addled, sleep-deprived brain that Penthouse Joan Parks was hitting on me. My jaw dropped and my fatigue cleared.

****

Joan Carolyn Parks and I were an item for seven months.

We talked each other's ears off. She was very well read and something of a poet and very romantic. I saw her as fearless, an adventurer.

One afternoon when our days off happened to coincide, she asked me if I had ever watched the movie "Camelot." When I said I hadn't, she scanned the newspaper and found a showing at a drive-in theater on the west side of town.

At dusk, we headed out in my 1965 Malibu convertible. I think it was the only time in my life that I actually watched a movie at a drive-in theater with a nice looking, single lady; the privacy of my own apartment was superior to that in the front seat of a car.
I was never much for musicals, but Joan wanted me to pay close attention as the two of us slowly munched on one small bag of

popcorn. The movie ended late, and we were both tired when we got back to our building. We kissed each other good night in the elevator.

I knew that tomorrow would bring questions about that movie.

"So, Michael," Joan said in my apartment the next day. "What do you think about Guinevere's decision to leave her beloved, good husband to go off with a knight in shining armor? Was she a rascal?"

"Oh, I think she broke her vow, and she was wrong," I said. "She obviously struggled with guilt."

When she didn't respond I said, "Joan Parks, what would you have done in her situation?"

"I'd like to think I would stay with my husband. But, honestly, I'd probably follow my heart rather than my head."

She frowned and looked into the distance. I loved her openness and willingness to discuss whatever weakness or strength came to mind. Joan knew she was a romantic; I think she felt that made her weak.

One day in Dave Coats's apartment, Dave looked at Joan and said, "I can see you as a pioneer wife in 1870 sitting bravely beside your man on a schooner headed to the West Coast. You just look strong and brave and willing to face anything. Totally unafraid."

Joan beamed and I nodded in agreement. I could easily picture her as Dave described.

I could talk to her about anything, and that was a new experience.

Through her own honesty, she taught me to be more open than I had ever been. Over time, I learned that she had been raised a Baptist in conservative Tennessee. She eventually drifted into a more liberal world. After completing her master's degree in nutrition, she lived in Europe and taught on American military bases. She wanted more of that kind of worldly life. Compassionate and sentimental, she worried about the little people—the poor and struggling—fearing the odds were stacked against them.

As I developed feelings for her, I realized I was wasting both her time and mine.

She was an adventurer and never wanted to be a housewife and raise kids. She was six years older than I was; her job paid about five times what I brought home.

I knew she cared for me, a guy who never finished college, but I also knew that what she really wanted was someone completely different—someone with whom I could not compete. She had told me this early in our relationship, not to hurt my feelings, but to state honestly what she sought in a spouse.

And now it was time to tell her I thought it best that we see others. She was hurt, but understood.

Neil Armstrong walked on the moon on the night in July when Joan and I were together for last time, dancing to Clair de Lune on her penthouse balcony under a bright, full moon.

Our relationship was book-ended with the successes of Apollo 8 and Apollo 11—somehow appropriate, I think, because she was a heavenly experience for me. I walked away much braver and more confident, unafraid of the ladies, thanks to her.

***

Every now and then Rod McKuen's "Love's Been Good to Me" will come over the radio. The reference to a girl in Denver always makes me think of Joan.

Forty-four years after we parted, I was shocked to see obituaries for Joan's two Denver roommates. Both had succumbed to cancer, and I suddenly needed to know about Joan. With the help of the internet I tracked her down and called her.

We became friends once again, this time via telephone and long emails. She told me that in her first marriage she and her husband built a sailboat, sold all they owned, and sailed from California to the East Coast via the Panama Canal.

When the marriage ended, she returned to Knoxville, where she bought and ran an art gallery and frame shop for thirty-five years. Her second husband, as well as her first, had doctoral degrees. She got what she wanted in terms of a spouse, and in our correspondence she repeatedly told me she was a lucky woman.

We met in person once, when my wife Jane and I had dinner in San Antonio with Joan and a group of her long-time Tennessee lady friends who were on a road trip together.

Joan was always interested in spirituality and religions. As we exchanged thoughts and ideas, she intimated that maybe she and I knew each other from another time or life. She liked to ponder things like that, as I do. Due to the spookiness of so many details that caused us to meet in the first place, I can't argue with her musings.

Five years after Joan and I re-connected, Joan surrendered to the cancer that had dogged her for several years.

Before she died, she sent good-bye notes to all her friends. I responded, but did not hear back. I miss her and her voice and her emails, and I still smile at her memory and the bravery and intelligence she showed me in this crazy life.

I once described our last dance to a talented poet and friend, Larry Bradfield. He came up with the lines below. I tinkered with it a tiny bit and here it is:

> He was raised near a West Texas sand dune.
> The honky-tonks and sawdust fit him well.
> Although partial to a Debussy tune,
> He was just as apt to cuss and raise hell.
>
> Then one day he went to Denver for good,
> Changed sand in his boots for views without end.
> He learned quickly, as he'd known that he would,
> Pretty girls lived in Penthouses, my friend.
>
> Joanie was smart and he knew that was right,
> Her Southern whispers met his Texas drawl.
> They danced as an Apollo moon shone bright,
> And marveled how young they had seen it all.
>
> What more was there than to dance Clair de Lune?
> All while men walked upon that big ol' moon.

CHAPTER 15

RECOGNIZING STABILITY

Jane Palmerton was a secretary to the director of flight training at Frontier Airlines. The dispatch office was at the other end of the hall, and every time I worked the day shift I saw her at her desk as I passed by. She never looked up from her work.

Slim, attractive, and serious, she was my age and wore no wedding ring.

The only copy machine on the floor was in the dispatch office, and occasionally Jane came into our all-male workspace with an armload of paperwork. The men teased any female who dared enter our little enclave, but Jane kept her eyes straight ahead, did her copying and left, having made no reply or eye contact with any of the lecherous males.

After Joan and I parted ways, I possessed a new confidence and outlook. One day in June 1969, I stopped by her office. She looked up with a neutral expression—not even a hint of curiosity—and said nothing, waiting for me to speak.

I introduced myself and asked her on a date for that Friday.

"I can't," she said. Then she just looked at me. I looked back but got no explanation.

"Uh, okay. How about Saturday?"

"I can't then, either."

I turned to leave.

"I'm in a musical both of those nights, but I could do something on Sunday after it's all over," she said. "We've been practicing for weeks. *The Mikado.*"

She wrote down her name, address, and phone and handed it to me with a slight smile. *This was going to be interesting.*

She worked around pilots and had plenty of opportunities to date, but I was curious about her. I was not fond of musicals, and I had no idea what a Mikado was, but I asked for some details and surprised her when I attended the Saturday performance.

We chatted after it was over, and she seemed pleased to see me.

I picked her up on Sunday and we ate boiled shrimp at a basement restaurant in historic Larimer Square in downtown Denver. Ironically, Cheryl and I had eaten there when I interviewed for the dispatcher's job. We might have sat at the same table, but that seemed like a lifetime ago.

Jane said she had never eaten boiled shrimp. Boy, did I feel worldly! On our second date we went to one of Denver's rare Mexican food places, another meal that was a first for her.

These Midwestern ladies were pretty square.

I learned she was from Rapid City, South Dakota, where her father was an ophthalmologist. She had majored in English at a small Baptist college in Sioux Falls. Her dad was on the college's board of regents and handed Jane her diploma when she walked across the stage at graduation.

We both loved knowing words, and she was reader, too. We enjoyed each other intellectually, but our backgrounds were so dissimilar I wondered if a long-term relationship would work. My schedule made it difficult to have a normal dating life, so we talked a lot on the phone. One evening we disagreed on something—I don't remember what—and I decided to end the relationship right then and there.

"Wait a minute," she said. "If we disagree, why can't we just work our way through it and sort it all out?"

I was floored.

Maybe I had discovered stability at last. Most importantly, it reinforced the profound advice I once received: open up and let people know who you are. Don't just walk away leaving others wondering what the heck you really want.

She was sharp as a razor and definitely not a drama queen who cried at the first hint of rejection from a suitor.

I decided to give this relationship more time.

* * *

One sunny Saturday afternoon some months later as we were sightseeing in the mountains, our stomachs told us it was time to eat. We got fried chicken at a small town drive-through and ate as we drove.

When I saw she liked the dark meat and I liked the white, I knew we meshed and took it as a prompt to propose.

It wasn't terribly romantic, and we both no doubt sported crumbs on our faces and grease on our fingers, but she accepted. We were married in June 1970 in her parents' living room in Rapid City.

As a married man, I wanted to get away from midnight shifts and limited income prospects. I had passed the written and oral exams for the dispatcher's license, so that goal was accomplished. Frontier gave me a paltry raise of three hundred dollars per year for the effort.

I was well aware that many people want the security of a steady paycheck. I once met a guy who told me, "I couldn't stand not knowing how much money was coming in that week." I came back with, "I couldn't stand knowing that no matter what I did, that was all that was coming in that week."

Not me. Not now.

I craved possibilities, not security. Not having a college degree limited my prospects, but I knew I wanted a career that had the potential to earn an income high enough for me to own an airplane.

Determined and much more confident, I thought I knew something that few others realize: we live in a world full of victims.

A motivational speaker once told me that if you want to succeed, you have to believe that the best thing you have going for yourself is your lousy competition, because most of them are victims who don't try hard at anything except getting attention.

***

I researched real estate sales and enrolled in a night course to get my Colorado real estate license. At the time, Colorado's exam for a license was reputedly the second-hardest in the nation. I passed on my first try and gave my notice to Frontier in October 1970.

I spent the next several months working for the largest residential real estate company in Denver, which happened to be Moore Realty. During the first week with Moore I was assigned to a desk in an office on the south side of Denver. For the first few days, I talked to the long-time agents and pored through the company policy and procedures manual. I also picked out one of the long-time producers and cornered him.

"If you were me, a new guy to town and to the business, what would you do to keep from failing at this game?" I asked him. Though I was no longer consumed by it, the fear of failure hadn't left me entirely.

He smiled and pondered for a moment.

"If I were you," he said, "I would go after the For Sale by Owners in this area. You can't just sit around and hope the phone will ring and a deal will fall in your lap. It doesn't work that way, and a lot of people who try that don't last long.

"When you talk to a "for sale by owner", remember: You have to find out why the homeowner is selling in the first place. If his motivation is greed, hoping his house is worth way more than it really is, don't fool with him. But if the owner truly has a plan and needs to sell but just doesn't like to pay a commission, then you decide in your own mind if the seller's motivation for selling is strong enough to correct the price when a contract comes in.

"If so, then tell him you think you can get what he wants plus your commission. The main thing is to get the listing! Put up a sign, and your phone will ring. It's that simple to begin with. Do that, and then come back and I'll tell you some more secrets."

***

The next morning I knocked on doors and talked to prospective sellers. In one week I got two listings.

I didn't have to wait long for my phone to ring. A woman wanted to know the price on one of my listings. She thought it was too high, but she wanted to make an offer on a different Moore listing.

"I want to write that contract, ma'am," I told her.

She said, "Okay, come on over. My husband and I are available at five thirty this afternoon. We want that house."

I excitedly told my sales manager about the conversation. He got a funny look on his face and said he had to go. I was euphoric about writing my first contract, but my euphoria went out like a closet light when my manager came back with a contract on the house I intended to sell.

I had to call my prospect with the bad news.

It was hard to realize that I couldn't trust my ambitious sales manager. Several agents in the office jumped on him for beating me out of a sale. The lesson I learned was that I shouldn't tell anyone what I was doing.

In less than two months I listed five properties, sold one, and sold four shares of a land syndication. The income made my old job look like a pauper's. I quickly hit my stride.

My plan worked better and faster than I ever imagined, but Denver was a red-hot market, and that helped tremendously; the name of the company didn't hurt, either! My managers and peers gave me many compliments on my performance.

The memory of my victim mentality faded, as if it existed only in a previous life.

***

My best friend, Alford Smallwood, and his wife Sarah Frances had moved from Odessa to Austin, at the edge of the Texas Hill Country I loved so much.

Jane and I visited and I had such a great feeling that I told Jane I wanted to live there.

Jane, the Midwesterner, got a stomach ache. She loved Denver. It was a day's drive to her parents' house and just a short hop in an airliner. Having been in Texas only once, she thought the state was like a foreign country where people ate *waterburgers* (she had misinterpreted my reference to "Whataburger") and enjoyed food so spicy it could burn the hair out of your nose.

Sarah's casual reference to "real foreign students, not just Yankees" did nothing to reassure her. But we were a team, and she would accompany me there if that's what I wanted to do.

When I saw that I was better than average as a real estate agent when I gave things my best shot, I gave Moore Realty my notice.

The office managers liked me and were surprised when I told them I was headed to Austin.

The agent who originally advised me on the for-sale-by-owner plan grinned and said, "You'll make it, Mike."

I think my sales manager blamed himself for my leaving. I never told him differently.

****

By March 1971 I was in Austin and employed with the state's largest private residential real estate builder and brokerage firm. Jane served out her thirty days' notice with Frontier and packed at the same time. I flew back to Denver, and the two of us drove her car to Texas.

In Austin, I took Jane to our new insurance agent's office and introduced her. The agent had spent his early life in Odessa, and we had an instant bond. When he asked Jane if she was looking for a job and she said she was, he said he might be able to help.

He listened carefully as she described her education and experience. The next day, Jane had an interview with State Farm Insurance, the nation's largest casualty insurance company, which was building a new regional headquarters in Austin. She was hired immediately as the secretary to the director of personnel, who was coordinating the hiring of employees for the new office.

I approached my job in Austin the way I did in Denver, giving my best and working long hours seven days a week. I thrived on it and picked the brains of the successful people I met.

My sister Shirley and her husband, my best friend Alford and Sarah, and a couple I knew from high school comprised the total number of people I knew in Austin. All three couples bought homes through another real estate agent rather than with me in 1971.

Gulp.

Still, I was named my company's New Salesman of the Year. I stumbled, I fell, and I failed at some things, but I viewed those missteps as part of the learning curve and not the end of the world.

Did the truths I discovered at twenty-five in Denver help me in my jobs? Without a doubt.

***

One evening when Jane and I were at Alford and Sarah's house, Sarah reminisced about our Odessa year and casually said that one of her fondest memories was celebrating a friend's birthday, Helen Joyce Wheeler, in the sand hills on their ranch west of Notrees.

I gasped, visibly rattled.

Sarah stopped talking in mid-sentence and asked what was wrong.

"Sarah, I was there!" I said. "I was one of those Boy Scouts watching all of you jet around in your underwear. It was the spring of our sixth grade year—1955."

In a flash, I realized the identities of all the girls I spied playing in the sand dunes so many decades earlier. I had gotten to know them in my junior high school days.

Sarah was one of them. I fell in love with two others: Nancy Leach and Julie Richards. My lifelong friend Kathy Bunch was there, too.

Funny, isn't it, how so many things seem connected in this mystical, mysterious life?

CHAPTER 16

DEAR OLD DAD

After nearly two years as a real estate agent in Austin, I got my broker's license and opened my own company with a partner.

We teamed with a local builder to form Thornton, Murphy and Moore Realty, and not only did we market Thornton's new homes, we aggressively went after the pre-owned market. Utilizing what I had learned and implementing some of my own ideas, we did well.

During the three years we worked together, I learned the steps of land development and how to leverage myself into deals I could put together only with the help of others who had the needed capital.

Jane was quickly promoted to executive secretary to the two deputy regional vice presidents at State Farm's new regional office: the director of operations and the director of agency. Her position opened the door for my introduction to the region's top three executives. They saw I was doing well and started dropping hints to Jane that I would make a good insurance agent for State Farm. The job required a college degree, which I did not have, so I didn't respond right away. I enjoyed the real estate business and the wheeling and dealing that went with it.

Our first child, Erik, was born in October 1973. One morning when Erik was about a year old, Jane was dressing him when she heard a car pull up in our driveway.

She looked out the window and said, "Mike, there's a car in our driveway, and an older man is getting out of it."

I walked into Erik's room, still messing with my necktie as I dressed for a meeting, and nearly fainted.

It was dear old Dad.

I hadn't seen or heard from him since he conned me out of fifteen dollars a decade earlier. I sometimes wondered if he was even alive, and here he was, first thing in the morning, in my driveway in a dirty, brown station wagon.

I gave up on my tie and went out to greet him. As I got close to him I could smell alcohol and see that he was drunk. A collection of empty bottles littered the inside of the car.

I had no spare time, and felt I had to keep this inebriated alcoholic away from my wife and son, for whom he was a total stranger.

My sister Shirley and her family lived just three doors down from us, so I steered him in that direction.

"Why don't you go see her and say hello," I said. "We can talk later."

He nodded dubiously as though he only half understood. He started his car and pulled away toward Shirley's house and I jumped into my own car and left for the day.

When I got home that afternoon, the station wagon was nowhere to be seen. I called Shirley. She had not seen him and was surprised to hear he was in the area. I went to bed that night wondering what had become of him. My dreams were interrupted when the phone rang at seven o'clock the next morning.

It was Dad, calling from the Williamson County jail. He had gotten a DWI charge and wanted me to get him released!

When he left my house the day before, he evidently headed north out of town, and a highway patrolman spotted him weaving down the highway. The patrolman later told me that he literally had to bump the station wagon off the highway to stop him, and when he asked Dad how much he had had to drink, Dad replied, "I don't know. I'm not through yet."

***

At the time, our sister Lea lived in Dallas, while Butch and Shirley both lived in Austin. Yet, when our dad hit town, it was Mike's driveway he sought out. When I directed him somewhere else, he left town and got a DWI, and whom did he call then? Not Butch, his favorite son. Not Shirley, his favorite daughter.

He called me, his least favorite.

He took my money, but never asked the others for a dime. Why? I suppose he did not want to insult or alienate them. He suspected I was not his son, so it was okay to insult and alienate me. Or he just knew I was soft hearted.

Like a fool, I made bail for him and brought him into our home to await sentencing. I resented the intrusion, but I tried to be cordial.

One chilly night as a fire flickered in the fireplace, we talked about those difficult years in the '50s and early '60s. I asked if he missed Mom.

"I never loved her," he said.

Taken aback, I asked why he married her.

With look on his face that indicated he was amazed at the question, he answered, "To take care of her."

"Don't you think someone who loved her could have done a better job?" I asked.

He flinched and stared at the floor. I feel sure that until that moment he thought of himself as a victim, forced into an unwanted marriage to a woman he didn't love. Now the look on his face told me that he suddenly realized that his unloved wife was the victim, not him.

Then a thought hit me.

If my dad never loved my mother, and married her only because she was pregnant, and he resented her for that, then what if his brother Lewis had feelings for my mother, and vice versa? What if my dad, Allen James Moore, truly believed his brother Lewis was my father, like he had drunkenly claimed that night when he humiliated Butch and me?

When Lewis was killed in World War II, did my dad assume he now had to take care of his dead brother's son, Michael Lewis? What if the marriage was such a mismatch that he became a drinker, and the drinking worsened after he was kicked out of his own house and went bankrupt?

It is not a stretch to conclude that his belief that I was not his child made him think of me as someone who owed him something. He would not offend the others, but he never had any reservations about offending me by treating me so differently from my siblings.

But I never asked.

He couldn't leave Austin until his DWI was adjudicated. His car had been impounded, and none of us would help him retrieve it because none of us had a lick of faith that it would help him. When his court day came, I told his lawyer that I would not pay a dime for his defense costs unless the lawyer pleaded with the judge to send my crazy old man to an alcoholic rehab center. He got ninety days in rehab, but was never serious about staying sober. I later learned that toward the end of his stay, he spent the weekends drinking with his buddies from rehab. The taxpayer's money and the pocket money I gave him went down the toilet again.

Dad hung around Austin for nearly a year after that, staying mostly with my brother or sister, and then one day he left for good on a Greyhound bus bound for Odessa. I didn't trust him nor did I miss him.

* * *

With a son in my life, I felt I had to work even harder, and I spent long hours trying to be a good provider. One evening when Erik was nearly two, Jane headed out of the house to attend a meeting, leaving the two of us alone together for the first time.

I was deeply rattled when Erik held out his little arms and begged her to come back. He started to cry, his heart breaking because momma was gone and he was with a stranger—*me.*

I sat in a recliner and held out my arms for him to come to me. He paused and stared. When he finally allowed me to pick him up, I put him on my chest and leaned back into the recliner while he sniffled and finally went to sleep.

With a tear in my own eye, I made a decision. I wanted a job that let me be a father that my son could know, a father he could trust and love.

Simply holding him that evening changed me forever. He wet his diaper and my shirt, but I didn't care. I didn't want to disturb him. He slept in my arms until Jane came home.

It was a life-changing event.

I decided to learn more about the insurance industry and what it might hold for me.

CHAPTER 17

A CAREER PATH, AT LAST

When the State Farm regional vice president was made aware that I was interested in becoming a State Farm agent, he talked to State Farm's CEO to get a waiver for my lack of a college degree.

I started my new career on June 1, 1975, four years after moving to the Austin area. It was eye-opening to get to know my fellow agents and the company I now worked for. Agents who worked hard and smart were rewarded with company trips if they met certain goals. They were supported by the best administrative help in the industry, by far. Morale was higher than any place I had ever worked.

According to a 1976 Wall Street Journal article, State Farm had the best sales force in the country. I did what the highly successful agents around me told me to do in order to be productive. My creed was to copy those who are successful and not reinvent the wheel.

The income potential I was looking for was there if I was willing to pay the price. State Farm had carefully examined my financial status and saw that I had sufficient resources to survive a tough two years with virtually no net income.

The pay for beginners like me was terrible, again! In the beginning, every penny I earned would not be enough the cover the monthly overhead for both our home and my new office. In a way, State Farm's offer was cruel, but I saw the sense in it, and this time a huge carrot dangled in front of me.

One reason I was able to take the job was that I had put together a valuable land deal with no investment of my own money, and it infused nearly twenty thousand dollars into our savings account. We had also acquired some rental properties, and with the timely sale of those appreciated properties we never had to touch our personal savings.

As a trainee agent I was assigned to an office in an old, established, west Austin neighborhood. It was a decent location, but I understood new growth from my real estate experience, and would have preferred an area where business would come to me rather than my having to chase clients down. It would be harder this way, but after two years I would no longer be a trainee, and I could then choose my own office location.

***

In the meantime, I had to give my absolute best in these two years or fail spectacularly—a depressing thought. When I asked myself what would make me undepressed, I trembled a bit at the answer: my own airplane.

But with my current income, how could I afford one? I suddenly knew how to do it.

I remembered that I knew two fellows who had hinted to me that they wanted to learn to fly.

I picked up the classified ads and as though it was meant to be, there was a forty-five hundred dollar Piper Tri-pacer for sale in Austin—the same plane I learned to fly in. My imagination went wild, fueled by five years of wheeling and dealing in real estate and successfully leveraging banks and other people's money.

I didn't want to deplete our savings, so I hatched a plan: one third of the cost of the advertised Tri-pacer was fifteen hundred dollars. I would withdraw that amount from our savings and put it into a certificate of deposit at a local bank. I would tell my two buddies who wanted to fly to do the same, adding their money to mine, and together we would own a forty-five hundred dollar certificate of deposit. (CD)

We would offer the CD to the bank as collateral in exchange for a loan to buy the airplane for the same amount. The interest rate on the loan would be for two percent more than what the CD was earning. Since the CD, not the airplane, was the collateral for the loan, we would have no monthly payments. The two-point spread between the CD and the loan equaled ninety dollars, or an expense of thirty dollars per year for each of us three partners to own the airplane in a partnership.

I didn't think we needed insurance on an amount we could afford to lose, so the only other cost was the tie-down fee at the Austin airport, which amounted to fifteen dollars per month split three ways. Total cost per person per year amounted to ninety dollars before the expenses for gas and maintenance.

I could own an airplane and tie it down for under eight dollars per month!

We put the deal together and I now had my own airplane, albeit in a partnership. I was elated.

The next consideration was how to afford to fly it, and my history of colitis. I took a physical and was told there was no evidence of colitis, not even scar tissue.

I now knew about thirty-two State Farm agents in and around Austin who made decent money, so I told them I had an airplane and could take them anywhere they wanted to go on short trips within the state if they would buy the gas. They quickly threw their hats into my ring, and I got to fly a number of them many times. I shuttled folks to Houston and back, and I made several flights to West Texas.

As a new agent, I was under pretty tight control by my manager. For this reason, I tried to keep what I was doing very low key, but it didn't work out that way.

I had owned the airplane, and been an agent, for three months when the local fixed base operator at Austin's Robert Mueller Airport called to tell me that the new tire had been installed on the nose wheel of my airplane.

I was not in the office, and my manager took the call. He almost had a heart attack. I said as little as possible when he relayed the message to me. He shook his head over and over and muttered something about never hearing of a trainee agent owning his own plane. This was in earshot of the other trainee, I thought I heard him snickering.

My income improved during my second year as a State Farm agent, and I reasoned that I could now afford a better airplane. Our partnership recruited a fourth partner, and we traded the Tri-pacer in on an eight-thousand dollar Cherokee 140.

Each of us put two thousand dollars into the CD, and suddenly we had a much newer, fancier airplane, capable of instrument flight, though none of us cared to fly in instrument conditions. Still, I considered that model of Cherokee a beautiful, underpowered wimp. I wanted to trade it for more horsepower when I could.

When I finished my two years as a trainee agent, I finally started making enough money to achieve my long-time goal: to own a heck of a nice airplane.

I found an eighteen thousand dollar Piper Dakota with an auto-pilot and a fully loaded panel—a powerful workhorse. We financed it the same way as the others. We had no payments except for the annual interest on the renewable loan, which amounted to ninety dollars per partner.

Our son Leighton was born in 1976, so we were now a family of four. With the Piper Dakota, we could visit Jane's parents in South Dakota for less money than the cost of airline tickets to fly us there.

Mission accomplished. Dream realized. I was euphoric every time I saw or flew that airplane.

***

Late one night in 1976, I received a call from my brother Butch, who told me that our dad had been killed by a drunk driver in Odessa. Drunk himself, Dad was walking along the highway when he was struck.

He lived by the bottle and died by the bottle. No one was surprised. His graveside service was a testament to his life. His four children shed not a tear. We had shed enough of them as kids.

My dad died a lonely man. He didn't know how to be kind and loving, and he knew nothing of the art of making others feel good about themselves. I hold no grudges. Instead, I feel sadness for all those who choose to self-destruct. For most of us, happiness is a choice.

After Dad's death I filed an insurance claim on the policy of the drunken driver. The settlement amounted to only twenty-five hundred dollars; the insurance company argued that because of his lifestyle, my father's life had no monetary value.

How could I argue?

My share of the insurance settlement was six hundred and twenty-five dollars. Butch claimed the entire amount was his because he needed the money. Shirley and I let him have our shares because he was in dire straits again. Lea told him to go to hell.

Butch used the funds to buy his wife a fancy microwave oven. Some things never change.

***

My State Farm career spanned thirty two years. The company allowed me to build my insurance agency in Round Rock, Texas, a perfect location because of an exploding population.

That agency provided me the means to put both of my sons through college without any debt on my part or student loans on theirs. It has given my wife Jane and me a comfortable retirement. And last but not least, it allowed me to own several airplanes over the years, giving me the utmost fun and satisfaction, though it was not all fun. There were some moments of terror.

The Texas Baptist Children's Home in Round Rock shelters youngsters whose parents are unable to properly care for them. I knew the feeling because of my own experience growing up, and Jane and I often made donations to TBCH to further their mission. I had never really had a mentor, and I approached the Home with the offer to mentor one of the students there by teaching him to fly my airplane and helping him build flying time toward a commercial license and a flight instructor's rating in order to earn money while in college.

Perry Potter was fifteen years old when I met him; I was told he had a photographic memory and could easily absorb information. In January of 1999 I took him for his first airplane ride. We flew for no more than one hour. He didn't touch the controls. Two months later when our schedules matched, Jane and I fed Perry a dinner at our home where I had a room dedicated to a table-top flight simulator that I had bought and used several years before to get my instrument rating. Perry was intrigued and asked to use it, and I gave him about fifteen minutes of instruction before Jane called out "Dinner's ready!" End of lesson.

It was May before Perry, now sixteen, and I flew again. I lifted off with Perry in the right seat. I told him to put his hands on the controls and his feet on the rudder pedals and to follow my motions. We climbed out and headed northwestward from the Georgetown, Texas, airport. It was an instruction ride, and I let him make climbing turns and then level off at altitude. I then showed him how to maintain altitude and hold a heading while scanning the flight and engine instruments. When we approached San Saba I took the controls and started a descent to buzz a remote ranch house that we once owned in partnership with friends, fellow insurance agents. They were there, and I passed over the house low, knowing the noise would flush them outside. I made a climbing wide turn to make another low pass. This time, they were out front when I came by again. They pointed in the direction of the local airport indicating they would pick us up there.

Perry and I landed and were taken to the ranch where we took him boat riding on the ranch's lake. They fed us lunch and then took us back to the airport. After take-off, I again let him have the controls. His focus was unrelenting. I was impressed with how smooth he was and how well he responded to instruction. When we entered the Georgetown airport area I took over the controls and landed the airplane while he watched me intently. By this time Perry knew our hangar's lock combination and he helped me put the airplane back in the hangar. We locked it up and I took him back to the Children's Home. He never practiced a take-off or a landing himself.

At eight o'clock on the morning of June 10th, 1999, I was on the phone with a friend when my answering machine showed I was getting a call from The Texas Baptist Children's Home. My stomach went into a knot and a foreboding feeling came over me as I quickly disconnected from the first call to answer the other. A stressed voice came over the line: "Mr. Moore, this is Perry Potter's cottage parent at the Children's Home. Perry and another boy have run away, and Perry has taken the aviation maps you gave him to study. We are scared to death he might try to do something with your airplane."

I told the house parent I would call her back. I immediately called the Georgetown Airport and asked for the manager. "Travis," I said, "I need you to go to my hangar and see if my airplane is there. I was warned that someone might steal it."

Travis called me back on his cell phone as he drove to my hangar. There was a short silence, then, "Mike, your airplane is gone."

I called the TBCH and told them. They called the police and then all hell started breaking loose. My cell phone started to melt down as I headed to the airport. A reporter for the Austin newspaper wanted the story, but I was getting another call and told him I would let him know. The waiting call was from a good friend with her own sense of humor: "I just heard over the radio that you are having a wonderful day. I will be thinking of you. Good-bye!" As soon as she hung up, the phone rang with a call from the Georgetown police department who wanted information and said they would meet me at the airport. We arrived at about the same time.

I filled out a form for the officer there that resulted in an all-points bulletin that sent the message to all law enforcement departments in Texas and other states. From there the story went worldwide.

The next call was from a TV station wanting an interview. They told me the story had already gone as far as Russia and Australia, and they were sending a man representing a TV station in Munich, Germany to do a documentary. My cell number was leaked and while I fielded more calls my airplane partner and his wife and daughter pulled up to the hangar. I told them the whole story as I knew it. He was silent for a while and I knew he was thinking the same thing I was: wreckage of the airplane was very likely nearby, smoking and crushed with two dead people in it.

 Just then the police officer's cell phone rang. When she hung up, she told us, "Your airplane is at the Brownwood, Texas, airport and it appears to be unharmed. They know where the kids are."

Relieved that the worst part of the story was over, my partner looked at me and said, "Mike, your intentions with that kid are very noble, but if you ever let that little son of a gun (not his actual words) near our plane again, I'll kill you." I understood.
I went straight to my office where my three employees stared at me unbelievingly. One said, "Mike, you have a phone call from the Los

Angeles Times on line two." Within the next hour I talked to the Fort Worth Star Telegram and the Houston Chronicle and two local TV stations who wanted to meet me at the airport in Georgetown. It was a long stressful day.

We learned that Perry and his buddy had sneaked out of the Children's home after midnight. They walked to a pay phone and called a cab to take them to the airport ten miles away. Though it was a dark overcast night, Perry took off the airplane and was reputedly headed to Colorado. He said he ran into bad weather, and he thought he took a lightning strike because he lost both GPS (navigational) units. He then made a U-Turn and started looking for runway lights. He landed at the Temple, Texas, airport and taxied to the ramp, all of this at night and without any practice. At dawn, workers arrived at the airport and the two boys got help with the GPS units and got them both working. Perry bought several dollars of fuel and took off again. No one there was even suspicious.

He was heard at Brownwood making a professional call-up for airport conditions. A flight instructor was in the traffic pattern with a student and watched my Piper Cherokee 235 make a nice landing. The two kids got out of the airplane and asked for the courtesy car. Neither had a driver's license, much less a pilot's license. Unlike at Temple, the Brownwood airport manager was highly alert and skeptical. These two guys had no whiskers.

The night watchman offered them a ride into town and dropped them off at a convenience store where they ordered breakfast. A Brownwood policeman who was also a pilot had rushed to the airport as soon as he got the all-points bulletin and was shocked to see the airplane there. The airport manager called the night watchman and learned where he had dropped the kids off. They were arrested and brought back to Georgetown.

We retrieved our airplane, and it was not damaged in any way. I was famous for a week with the news media and longer than that with some of my policyholders who thought the whole thing was hilarious. I thought it was another miracle in my life, but what do I know?

That was twenty-one years ago at this writing. It still fascinates me that a young beleaguered male would squander the opportunity I offered him. His actions proved that victims often choose self-destructive behaviors. Perry supposedly got to the Children's home as a victim by circumstance. He left the home as a victim by choice.

I offered him what I thought was a deal of a lifetime, a future, something I would love to have been offered to me when I had nothing as a teen. Instead, he played the victim card and lost it all.

***

Life has been good. I refuse to stay a victim every time something goes wrong.

It feels so good to know that you are giving life itself your best shot, and that alone keeps you out of the pity pot. I don't always win the battle, but if you keep on learning and trying again, failure is a figment of the imagination. I try to do my due diligence before jumping into something, even relationships. I am not flawless by a long shot, but I know how to escape the victim mentality when it creeps up on me. I avoid self-destructive habits and behaviors. I try constantly to make others feel good about themselves.
When I was close to retirement, my manager called me to the front of an agents' meeting.

"It gives me great pleasure to present this award, because so few qualify for it," he said. "Mike Moore, this one is yours."

It was an award for agents who consistently made the company a profit in all lines of insurance over the years. The honor is reserved for less than one percent of State Farm's eighteen-thousand-strong workforce.

The applause of my peers was music in my ears.

Most of my awards have been set aside, but I have kept that one and the one naming me new salesman of the year when I was starting out in real estate. They represent the beginning and end of my careers. I think I gave both careers my best. It worked.

I retired in 2007 at age sixty-four. My working career was a real rocket ride. Jane and I did things and traveled places with State Farm that we never would have done or seen otherwise.

I eventually had to quit flying due to fights with the FAA and my doctors over my diabetes. I sold my last airplane in 2013 and cried like a baby. I am not bitter because I feel so lucky for having experienced a life with airplanes in it.

I am grateful.

CHAPTER 18

THE AUTHENTIC SELF

"It is usually quite difficult for the victim to come to see that he or she is living out of the victim identity instead of living from the authentic self, because there is shame attached to their efforts to manipulate and their history of failures. But if he can come to see it clearly and hear the messages it gives him, he can begin to recognize that this mask and costume was never real in the first place, and that there is someone within who is strong and capable and on whom he can rely."

~~ Andrea Mathews LPC, NCC

Years ago, I heard a talk at a symposium of psychologists in Austin. One speaker talked about a study that claimed that all of human behavior is aimed at one thing only: validation of self.

After his presentation, I told the speaker that I thought he had just destroyed about two hundred years or more of psychology and psychiatric theories with one premise. Perhaps Mr. Rogers said what we all long to hear: "I like you just the way you are."

After decades of the concept simmering in my brain, I have concluded that the quest for validation is directly connected to the thought process that leads to the victim mentality.

I think it is axiomatic that when someone is not validated in the way he or she expects, that person automatically has to choose how to deal with the perceived rejection: to be a victim or not be a victim.

To choose the victim path is to choose self-destruction and loss of control of your own life and talents. To choose not to be a victim is to press onward and give life your best. That is what it means to be your true, dependable self.

One way to give life your best is to make others feel good about themselves, thus validating them and fulfilling their strongest emotional need.

I once read an article in a golf magazine—not a textbook on psychology or psychiatry!—that taught me one of the most important things I have ever learned. I have not been able to track down the article to give credit. It was about an encounter the author had with Arnold Palmer during a golf tournament. I'll call the author Bob.

Palmer recognized Bob as they approached each other on the cart path. With a big grin, Palmer extended his hand and they stopped to chat. Palmer asked Bob how his life was going, but as he answered, Bob noticed that he'd lost eye contact with the King of Golf, who was looking over Bob's shoulder at a nice looking young lady coming up the cart path afoot. She stopped and hooked her arm into Bob's arm and smiled pleasantly at them both.

"Palmer," Bob said, "meet my new wife, Mia!"

As they concluded their conversation, Palmer shook their hands and looked at Bob saying, "Hey Bob! Good job!" Palmer then winked and nodded toward Bob's wife, complimenting Bob's choice. He then continued walking, hitching up his pants in his trademark fashion.

Bob watched the famous golfer walk away when this thought flashed into his mind: "I now realize why everyone loves Palmer. Palmer makes everyone he meets feel good about themselves!"

Surely what Palmer taught Bob is an acquirable skill for nearly everyone. I believe this because I've tried to do it myself. Sometimes I forget and get frustrated with people, but Palmer's secret is an easily-proven hypothesis and indisputably beneficial philosophy. How simple and beautiful—yet elusive—it is until someone articulates it.

Making others feel good about themselves is the key to developing our own self-validation, and it also seems to aid in the solving of many inner conflicts.

In my own example, my lowest point in life, the "poor you" moment," was instantly followed by my "eureka moment." In that magical instant I was made to see that in my past, several others had made me feel good about myself.

The circumstances of my early years mostly boil down to a father who didn't have a clue how to love or raise his children. After his wife, our mother, died, he didn't know how to support himself, and he abandoned three teens, leaving us homeless and surviving only through the charity of others until we could make it on our own as adults. It was not easy.

I survived by getting away from him and finding inspiration in those around me who sought to do something positive with their lives.

As a struggling teen, I was rescued by my best friend Alford Smallwood and by Cameron Ray's mother, Willie Beth Ray, because they thought I had value. I owed it to them and multiple others who I knew cared for me to give my life my best shot.

I believe the harm that the victim mentality brings to our lives needs more attention, and this tale is the best I can do to try to pass on what I have learned. My best, simple advice is this:

Recognize that the victim is a fearful and unhappy human.
Choosing to stay a victim is a destructive waste of life and a poor survival technique.
Giving life your best shot is the best survival technique.
Make others feel good about themselves.

In my opinion, nowhere is the avoidance of the victim mentality better illustrated than in the auto-biography of William Kamkwamba. He was THE BOY WHO HARNESSED THE WIND and that is the title of his book. As an uneducated boy genius in Africa he brought electricity and modernity to his home country. His message is that if you want something bad enough, just try hard and don't give up, instead of waiting for someone to do it for you. His autobiography should be mandatory reading. In a time where there are few unselfish heroes, he is a giant amongst us, in my opinion.

CHAPTER 19

SOME WORDS ABOUT MY PASSION: NEUROFEEDBACK

I have a soft spot in my heart for people with learning disabilities and brain disorders. They are the some of the world's true victims through no fault of their own, and society doesn't have a clue about how to help them. Many of them make poor decisions that profoundly affect them and those around them, but they don't play this game of life with a full deck of cards. They often run afoul of the law, spending their lives entangled in the criminal justice system, many ending up in prison because the system does not know what to do with them. They are often estranged from family and friends. Many homeless people are brain disordered in some way.

My father destroyed his life with alcohol. My more educated guess is that my dad was probably dyslexic, and from his behavior swings I suspect he was also bipolar. Understanding that my father was a true victim has allowed me to forgive him. How could I hate him? My only option was to forgive him for the pain he caused. Forgiveness freed me from my anger toward him, and once again, I felt the glorious freedom of no longer believing I was a victim, unable to change myself or my circumstances.

I believe his struggles stressed him to the point that he felt he had to drink in order to forget his inner demons. It is easy to say he quit learning, but maybe he couldn't learn like most people.

If my guess about my father's brain is correct, he was a tortured human being. During a talk we had late in his life when he was in one of his reflective moods, he hung his head sadly and told me, "No one knows the troubles I've had."

In my heart, I believe he was talking about his internal struggles with the limitations that made him feel insecure, inferior, and rejected.

***

I was a lousy student, especially after my elementary school years. Growing up, I blamed my poor study habits on my social life and chaotic family life. I thought I was just distracted. I would often read a whole page of text and realize I had no idea what I had just read.

The truth is, however, that my straying mind was a classic symptom of attention deficit disorder (ADD), a condition that was not recognized at the time. I now believe that my attention deficit disorder originated with an incident when I was eleven years old.

Before my family melted down completely, our favorite vacation spot was Lake Buchanan, near Austin. We visited that lake several times during the summers from 1953 through 1957.

One summer I was so excited about a return to that body of water that I wore my swim trunks under my jeans for the five-hour drive from Odessa. When we arrived, I stripped down to my trunks and ran for the dock where I had spent so many hours the summer before. I dove head first off the end of the dock, not noticing that the water level was much lower than during our previous visits.

I hit my forehead on the bottom and nearly knocked myself out. Though it hurt like crazy and I was dizzy, I managed to pull myself onto the dock and lay there until I felt better. I remember thinking that I could have been badly hurt.

No one was watching, and I said nothing about it. Finally my head cleared enough that I felt fairly normal, and the rest of the week didn't reveal any lasting effects.

In retrospect, however, I associate that injury with my focus problems later on.

In the summer of 1966, when I got the opportunity to learn how to fly, one of my biggest concerns was whether I would be able to focus enough to avoid a fatal error. One of the requirements to get a private pilot's license was at least five hours of instruction while under a hood, practicing instrument flight with no outside visual flying cues.

Instrument flying is the most difficult part of a pilot's job. My first day of instrument instruction was extremely mentally rigorous. I knew I had to concentrate every moment, to constantly scan all the instruments while maneuvering the airplane, always thinking ahead.

At the end of the first lesson in instrument flying, I was exhausted, and I realized my forehead was stinging, and I had a slight headache.

The next day I experienced the same thing. The third day was easier, and I began to enjoy instrument flying. I no longer felt the stinging sensation.

Studying became easier, too. I could stay at it for hours, like never before. Something had changed for me with that stinging sensation. That "something" came to me years later while I was sitting in on a high-level lecture about the human brain.

***

While he was a toddler and again when he was in grade school, our younger son, Leighton, took some unfortunate blows to his head. When he was thirteen, we took him to a neurologist because we saw that he had trouble studying and had some behavioral issues. That is when I first learned about Attention Deficit Disorder.

The statistics are horrifying. Those with ADD have more broken marriages and a higher suicide rate. ADD children have a sixty percent chance of getting involved in the legal system. I knew I had to fight for my son's life.

I've always been an obsessive reader, and I dove into all the books I could find on the subject. They all boiled down to two things: no one knew what causes it, and no one knew how to treat it other than with talk therapy and drugs that had never been tested on children.

We tried them all with no success. As a family, we struggled with fears about our son's future. We knew he was smart, but he was barely passing his high school classes, and did not want to go to college.

He had fallen into the traps of ADD.

***

I was determined to find someone who could tell me more than just bad news. In 1994, when Leighton was in his last semester of high school, I got a call from a friend, Dr. Jerome "Jerry" Schmidt, a clinical psychologist and family counselor in Austin.

What he said was magic: "Mike, I recently spent a week of training at the Menninger Clinic in Kansas where I learned about electroencephalogram biofeedback (later termed neurofeedback.) This stuff has the potential of remediating the symptoms of ADD. Come to my office and let me show you what we're doing."

Jerry was working with a freshman at the University of Texas at Austin. The young man was raised and schooled in a small town. He was a track star in high school and had an athletic scholarship to UT.

"I think I got through high school on my athletic ability and my good looks," he told me with a laugh. "But when I got to UT I was stunned at how hard all my courses were. My first semester I flunked everything except physical education, and now I'm on scholastic probation. One of my instructors assigned me to write a paper on attention deficit disorder, and now I know why.

"I recognized myself in everything I read about it. I went home one weekend and told my folks what I had learned and that I wanted help. They advised me to talk to my professor, and that is where I learned about Dr. Schmidt. I've had more than ten sessions, and I can already tell a difference compared to when I started. I love this stuff! I feel like now I know how to focus."

Jerry hooked the student up to an electroencephalogram (EEG) unit using two electrodes: one on the top center of his head that sensed his brainwave activity and another clipped to his ear to act as a ground. The EEG unit was connected to a computer that sorted the brainwave information into readable data which was displayed on the therapist's screen. The goal was for the student to increase the brain wave frequencies that represent the state of focus and to decrease the frequencies that represent stress.

The student sat in front of a second computer screen that had a Pac-Man game on it. He was told to relax and breathe normally. The main computer was programmed to make Pac-Man eat energy pills when the student's brain waves indicated he had reached the focus state. In other words, when the patient's brain produced evidence of focus, he was rewarded with the view of Pac-Man eating energy pills on his computer screen.

The ADD brain has difficulty maintaining the state of focus. The exercise taught the student what it feels like to stay focused, thereby conditioning his brain. Jerry's client, the student, felt he had his ADD in remission, and he was ecstatic.

So was I. I told Jerry that I wanted to learn all I could about this stuff.

Jerry chuckled as though he knew I would say that and told me about a week-long program in Los Angeles the next month. I fought back tears of relief. I felt our lives were changing.

***

I got a dictionary and a notebook and went to the conference, where I was the least-educated person in attendance. There was a psychiatrist, and many Ph.D.'s in psychology and neurosciences; there was a nurse who was married to and employed by a doctor, and many others.

It was one of the most exciting weeks in my life. Every day there gave me hope for my son.

The first lecture was presented by Dr. Barry Sterman, a neuroscientist, and Dr. Siegfried Othmer, a physicist. Sterman related how through his work with cats he discovered the brainwave frequency of focus, which he called sensory motor rhythm, or SMR.

Othmer and his wife Susan, a neurophysiologist by training, had children with serious brain issues. When they learned of Sterman's work they decided to learn all they could. The Othmers used Sterman's protocol to help their children mitigate seizures and modify behaviors. It worked better than any other efforts and they wanted the world to know what they had helped to discover.

I raised my hand and said, "I am a pilot and it seems to me that instrument flying, which requires intense concentration, would accomplish the same thing you are doing with this biofeedback protocol. Am I right?"

Sterman thought a moment and said, "I think that is quite possible."

Layman though I am, I was sure of it.

I had experienced it. Mental focus is attained via the front part of the brain, the cortex. The brain, including the cortex, is supplied with blood that nourishes the cells through tiny vessels called capillaries. Seemingly minor head injuries can compress or damage capillaries and diminish blood supply to that portion of the brain.

Those lectures taught me that the brain is remarkably resilient, and capillaries can apparently be regenerated and a healthy blood supply re-established through forced concentration such as I experienced with flight instrument training or via the proper biofeedback protocol, as I witnessed in Jerry Schmidt's office.

Hope now replaced my fear for Leighton's future. I was ecstatic.

Some of the therapists related that a few of their patients had reported a stinging sensation on their heads after treatment. I immediately thought of my own experience when I was first learning instrument flying.

After years of following the field of neurology, I now believe I damaged the capillaries in my brain at age eleven when I hit my head on the bottom of the lake, thus diminishing my ability to focus.

The week I spent in Los Angeles gave me a new direction in my life, another purpose. I now saw a way to potentially help my son and others in their efforts to remediate their deficits of attention.

***

When I returned home I immediately enrolled my son, a senior in high school with marginal grades, in a course of neurofeedback treatments, which he didn't finish.

Eighteen years old, he lacked confidence in his academic ability and loafed away most of the summer after he graduated from high school. A stint in Colorado, where he hoped to be a ski instructor, ended with a bad roommate experience and lack of funds, and he returned home late in the fall with a decision to give community college a try in the spring.

Again, he did not do well in school, and he made some poor choices that resulted in a legal entanglement. When he asked us for help, we agreed only if he finished the neurotherapy sessions he had abandoned several months before. He subsequently completed a total of about forty treatments.

He enrolled at a college far from his local friends and activities. It was from there that I received a phone call that made me weep with relief.

"Dad," Leighton told me, "for the first time in my life I am sitting in a math class completely absorbing everything the teacher is saying without it blowing past my head in a blur."

His words signaled to me that he would make it now. He could focus. I now knew he was headed toward the goal of self-confidence instead of the torture of personal defeat.

Intensely curious, I asked how he learned to control the Pac-Mac simulator.

He recalled the vicious murders of workers in a retail store years earlier that had horrified the community.

"One day during a treatment I visualized saving those girls. I was sword fighting and defeating the bad guys, and when I saw those scenes in my mind, Pac-Man took off on the computer screen."

I had never heard a scientific definition of focus in relation to learning disabilities. My son defined it for me with his story.

I concluded that focus is the conscious imaging of one's thoughts. I believe that imaging causes the brain to work to solve whatever problem is being addressed, and that the brain's memory of the imaging process is what allows the brain to train itself to focus.

I wanted to tell the world. But I was a nobody, and I had no credentials.

I chose to help more therapists enter the field and try to influence them.

***

I funded and started a clinic in my office building with Jerome Schmidt as a partner. That clinic is still open at the time of this writing, under different ownership.

Another businessman and I bought state-of-the-art equipment for a clinic in Georgetown, Texas. That clinic still exists, as well. I helped a psychologist in New Braunfels integrate neurofeedback into her practice.

There are other examples, too. My point is that I gave it my best shot by helping therapists and directing my friends and their friends to treatment centers.

And I am not finished.

Today, the EEG-biofeedback treatment is called neurofeedback. When I attended those lectures in 1994, there were fewer than two hundred neurofeedback practitioners in the United States. At the time of this writing, their numbers are in the tens of thousands worldwide and growing. In addition, the internet is full of information.

Neurofeedback is not a panacea, but in my opinion it is a step in the right direction. Some of the results of treatments have been spectacular.

Neurofeedback treatment has a failure rate, as well. Some people feel that being hooked up to a computer with electrodes on their scalp means that something is being done to their brain. I suspect that many people who see no benefit from neurofeedback don't quite understand that the computer and electrodes are not doing anything to them; success depends upon their own proactive output: they control the computer, not the other way around. An alert therapist is important.

Critics cite the lack of scientific data to support or dismiss claims made by therapists and patients. And while the plural of anecdote is not data, I join those who say that the results speak for themselves. It worked for my son and many others.

Leighton graduated from Texas State University with a degree in business administration. When he was finally able to get serious about the course of his life, he gave it all he had.

I'm convinced that neurofeedback played a huge role in his change of attitude and gave him the confidence he needed to be successful. Not only is he able to stay focused, he is now thought of as a guy who thinks outside the box.

***

One final story.

A longtime friend whose two sons went through neurofeedback with remarkable success subsequently asked me to talk to his sister, whose daughter was chronically depressed.

The thirty-two-year-old daughter had been in talk therapy for ten years and had not improved. I suggested she see Dr. Jonathan Walker,

a neurologist in Dallas.
Two significant things happened.

First, once she discovered how to meet the goals set for her in neurofeedback, she was able to briefly escape her depression.

"Do people feel like this all the time?" she asked in amazement.

Second, the physician, recognizing that there were emotional issues that he was not qualified to address, eventually released her, saying he and his team had done all they could do for her.

Not understanding why, the girl and her mother called me.

I advised them to use the "five whys" technique to drill down to the core issue. First, she should ask herself why she was depressed, then ask "why" again until the foundational answer is discovered. If she needed help, I said, they should ask the girl's therapist.

The girl discovered that she had been living under a false belief about her intelligence. She thought she allowed a tragic situation to occur and thus was not intelligent, when in fact she was the victim, not the perpetrator. Freed from this, she went back to college and graduated summa cum laude.

 Now that is real change, and I believe it came with the help of neurofeedback.

****

I believe most people who study the neurosciences are truly looking for ways to change lives for the better.

Other than deciding not to live my life as a victim, I believe that neurofeedback has been the most effective means of changing behavior that I—as well as many of my family members and friends—have experienced.

Furthermore, it is my opinion that most of those who engage in self-destructive or criminal behavior make their bad decisions as a result of a brain that is supercharged with the emotion of fear, which incorporates the emotion of anger.

They respond to feelings of rejection with violence. I believe neurofeedback quiets fear and allows rational thinking that can change these behaviors.

As neurofeedback grows, more resources are available. Two outstanding books are *The Emotional Brain: The Mysterious Underpinnings of Emotional Life*, by Joseph Ledoux, M.D., and *A Symphony in the Brain: The Evolution of the New Brain Wave Biofeedback*, by Jim Robbins.

It seems that nearly every family has a connection to someone with some kind of brain or personality disorder. Learning about neurofeedback might send you or someone you love on a real learning adventure.

The bottom line is that I believe that neurofeedback has changed the lives of many people I have known.

Mine included.

In closing, it should be apparent to any reader that over my earlier years I was vexed by a lack of confidence. I was haunted by the fact that maybe I was not as smart as I needed to be. Thank Goodness that thought disappeared for me.

What matters the most is not talent and intelligence; the most important things in life are self-discipline, grit and your own unique creativity. I have seen several talented geniuses wreck their lives with destructive behaviors and lack of self-discipline. In contrast, I met many highly successful people who attained their lofty goals because of hard work and perseverance rather than exceptional talents and I.Q.

No matter what age you are, it is a short life; don't waste it by being a victim. Just being is in itself potential. We were born to develop that potential.

ABOUT THE AUTHOR

Michael Lewis Moore was born in 1943 and was raised in the oil patch in west Texas. He left Odessa, Texas and the oil patch at age twenty-one and experienced environmental shock when he moved to Houston to further his education, which was interrupted by an opportunity to become a commercial pilot. Flying became his passion. After two years as a civilian flight instructor training Air Force students, he took a position as an aircraft dispatcher for an airline in Denver, hoping to eventually be hired as a pilot—which did not happen. After three years in Denver, he gave up aviation as a living but not as a passion. He spent five years in the real estate business in Austin, Texas, before he moved to a career as an insurance agent in Round Rock, Texas. His thirty-two year career in insurance allowed him to fly his own airplanes, and it also satisfied his interest in real estate. As of 2020 he will have been married to the same woman for fifty years; they raised two sons who graduated from college and are now out of their parents' pocketbook. The boys have provided two granddaughters, one each. Mike's wife Jane has been his editor and partner in all his madness. They have traveled a good deal over the years and are grateful for the life they've had together. This memoir is his first effort at publication.

The way we were